With a Taiko Glossary
by David Leong

Photographs by Francisco Villaflor,
X2 Digital Photography, Irvin Yamada, Max
Aguilera-Hellweg, Martin Butler, Lia Chang,
Robert Mizono, Kallan Nishimoto, Kumiko
Tanaka, Raymond Yuen

THE WAY OF
TAIKO

Heidi Varian

Foreword by
Seiichi Tanaka

Stone Bridge Press
Berkeley, California

Published by
Stone Bridge Press
P.O. Box 8208
Berkeley, CA 94707
tel 510-524-8732 • sbp@stonebridge.com • www.stonebridge.com

Cover photograph by Robert Mizono.

Part-title and title-page photographs by Francisco Villaflor.

Instrument photographs provided by Miyamoto Unosuke Shoten, Tokyo, except for photograph of *tetsu-zutsu* provided by Jay Mochizuki, Mochizuki Taiko Manufacturing Company. All other credits appear with their respective photographs.

Gatefold illustrations by Kumiko Tanaka.

All photographs and illustrations in this book are protected by copyright and may not be reproduced without the express permission of their rightsholders.

Taiko Glossary by David Leong used by permission and edited for this publication.

Cover, text design, and additional line drawings by Linda Ronan.

Printed in the United States.

2010 2009 2008 2007 2006 2005   10 9 8 7 6 5 4 3 2 1

LIBRARY OF CONGRESS CATALOGING-IN-PUBLICATION DATA
Varian, Heidi.
 The way of taiko / Heidi Varian ; with a taiko glossary by David Leong.
   p. cm.
 ISBN-13: 978-1-880656-99-0
 1. Taiko—History. 2. Taiko (Percussion ensemble)—History. 3. Taiko—Instruction and study. I. Title.
ML1038.T35V37 2005
786.9'0952–dc22

2005025122

This book is dedicated
To my husband David Gonzalez
To my children Tyler, Delsin, and Kenai for bringing joy to my every day
To my late father Harold "Tork" Torkelson and mother Dorothy Torkelson
And to the taiko community

Contents

Foreword by Seiichi Tanaka

When I founded the San Francisco Taiko Dojo in 1968, the first Japanese drumming performance group in the United States, I literally had to blaze a path through what I refer to as "the Taiko Frontier." During those early years, I felt as if the newly formed dojo and I were struggling in absolute darkness, but I held firm to the belief that if we didn't always strive to walk toward the sun, we would never become illuminated. Applying this attitude to the art of taiko meant seeking its very essence through a pure and strong sound. My dedication to taiko has led many of my friends, family, and former dojo members to think of me as "taiko crazy." While this apparent insanity has helped to fuel my passion for taiko, it has never lessened my appreciation for all of their support and wise counsel.

Back in 1968, karate and judo were already popular and well known outside Japan. Even back then, the names of these martial arts were a part of the English vocabulary. Not so with the word "taiko." From the very beginning, I had to follow a frontier spirit through the wilderness of the American desert, planting and cultivating the seeds of taiko.

My dream was only for the day when the drum would gain acceptance in America and become a form of music appreciated by everyone around the world. Today, the mature plants are bearing fruit throughout the United States and Canada. As an artist, and founder, this fills me with great joy. I am delighted and proud that some of my students have become, in their own right, top-level taiko artists, soloists, group leaders, and teachers of taiko here in the United States, Japan, and abroad.

The essence of taiko at the Taiko Dojo is based on the disciplines of spirit, action, body, and etiquette, or what I call "the Tanaka spirit and policy." Japan, the

ROBERT MIZONO, COURTESY SFTD.

Grandmaster Seiichi Tanaka.

birthplace of taiko, has experienced rapid economic growth, and everyone's need for food, shelter, and clothing has been fulfilled. The diet has become westernized, and the value of Japanese culture is being sadly forgotten. As a result, the Spartan concept behind the phrase *ore ni tsuite koi* (follow me and I will teach you) has almost died in Japan.

Taiko Dojo is the only internationally represented group in the United States to follow this austere concept. Even leading Japanese taiko groups are impressed that this method has produced such excellent results, and their reactions fill me with great pride. The future of taiko depends on the American taiko community coming together in understanding. It is my hope that this book will act as an introduction to my teachings—for taiko players, musicians, and music lovers alike.

After all these years, I feel as if Taiko Dojo is still on the road, climbing the mountain path, knowing our final destination is somewhere up ahead. As long as we do not forget what it was like when we started climbing, we will always be mindful of what has been accomplished. When we are on stage, we do the best that we can and make every performance as perfect as possible. We attain this goal with spirit—the idea being that each time we do something, it will be for our first and last time. This is the concept of *ichigo ichie*; we must do it right, here and now.

May this book guide you on your own journey of self-discovery.

SEIICHI TANAKA
Founder and Director
San Francisco Taiko Dojo

Preface

When I first saw taiko, I was moved by its intensity. Every beat was in the moment. The concentration and the emotional power of the performers were tantamount to their skill. That's what I enjoyed about it. Doing it myself never crossed my mind. Not once.

You see, those were the days when San Francisco Taiko Dojo practiced in the basement of the Japantown YMCA, back in the 1980s. It was a glorified storage closet, with asbestos ceiling fragments coming down with the vibration of the beats. Excellent form could knock out the hanging light bulbs. The small room smelled of sweat and blood from the rigorous training of Seiichi Tanaka. The drummers beat on tires. The actual drums were too honored and expensive and were only played in performance.

I was only there to pick up my friend who was a part of the dojo. After many appearances at the dojo, picking up or dropping off the group on tours and generally lending a hand (due to my proximity), I was invited by Seiichi Tanaka to join the ensemble. Of course, I declined. Repeatedly. It was never a question of cultural background, for even though taiko is a traditional Japanese art, Seiichi Tanaka's group is multicultural, to symbolize his belief in "Frontier Spirit." It was because it looked completely out of my league. I was a runway model, did some TV. I certainly didn't feel powerful and intense. I don't know what changed my mind, but one day I believed Sensei Tanaka when he said, "You can do this."

The most amazing part of taiko comes when you reach your limit and pass beyond it. Sensei Tanaka is a difficult teacher and one that many fear, for his dreaded "Tanaka style." But he is observant of all his students, always testing them, whether

MAX AGUILERA-HELLWEG

Heidi Varian.

they know it or not. The dojo is his life, his family, his world. He pushes his students further than they can go, to reach a goal that he can see. Maybe you, the student, cannot.

Taiko has taught me more than Japanese drumming and traditions. It has taught me focus and concentration. From the study of taiko, I learned humility, and also pride. In my years with Seiichi Tanaka and San Francisco Taiko Dojo, I have toured Europe, America, and Japan. I was the first woman and non-Japanese to perform the Norito (sacred prayer) at the Suwa Shrine in Japan. I have appeared in films, on national television, in magazines, on radio, and in a book. I have taught taiko as therapy to disabled children and adults. I have taught in correctional institutions. I have taught preschoolers. I have built in-

struments, made regalia, helped to create new ensembles. I still play in school assemblies regularly. I have passed many limits, but there are always new challenges, and I am always a student. I am no expert, I only have experience.

Taiko is a defining part of my life. I treasure the many wonderful friends I have made over the years in the taiko community. Everyone in my family plays taiko. I am Icelandic, my husband Aztec, and we are often asked why we play Japanese drums. I respond that if you try it, you would feel the connection. I owe a debt of gratitude to Seiichi Tanaka for teaching and encouraging me. Therefore, I try to keep my taiko standards high and the integrity of the art undiminished, and I always challenge myself.

I hope here to provide an accurate source of information, a book that brings many taiko ideas together in one place. Peter Goodman and Stone Bridge Press provided a great opportunity for taiko aficionados. It is a wonderful art, and I would like to encourage people to share that vision in the right ways. But I hasten to remind future practitioners that this is only a book and not a substitute for actual experience: "Do not mistake the finger pointing at the moon for the moon itself."

The taiko community is my second family, and the future of American taiko is important to me. The creation of this book was suggested by Seiichi Tanaka and Roy Hirabayashi and encouraged by my husband, David Gonzalez. But it is due to an ABC Preschool taiko student, whose mother, Ayako, forged the publishing relationship, that this volume even exists. It is my hope that I have stayed true to the community vision and that of the future. If you are inspired to taiko, remember: "You can do this."

Ganbatte,
Heidi

Acknowledgments

Many people and organizations in the taiko community generously helped in the creation of this book. I am grateful to them all and would like to thank the following in particular, with apologies if I have left anyone out.

Instructors: Grandmaster Seiichi Tanaka, Grandmaster Daihachi Oguchi, Seido Kobayashi, Kiyonari Tosha, Kenny Endo.

San Francisco Taiko Dojo: Kumiko Tanaka, Ryuma Tanaka, Nosuke Akiyama, Leigh Sata, Sarita Escobar, Ian Hadley, and everyone else.

Sponsors: Asano Taiko Ten, Miyamoto Unosuke and Miyamoto Unosuke Shoten, Miyamoto Yoshihiko, Jay Mochizuki, Nippon Taiko Foundation, Remo, Inc.

Supporters: Bridge Media, John Chasuk and Francesca Kirkpatrick, Jim Seff and Cydney Tune, Pillsbury Winthrop.

Contributors: Brenda Wong Aoki, Gisela Getty, Roy and PJ Hirabayashi, Etsuo Hongo, Joyce Nakada Kim, Masao Kodani and George Abe, Kodo, Hiroshi Koshiyama and Naomi Guilbert, David Leong and Rolling Thunder. Marco Lienhard, Jeanne Mercer and Russel Baba, Johnny Mori, Megumi Ochi and the Nippon Taiko Museum, Alan and Merle Okada, Stan Shikuma, Tiffany Tamaribuchi, Brian Yamami.

Photographers: Francisco Villaflor, Melvin Higashi and Ronald Young of X2 Digital Photography, Irvin Yamada, Max Aguilera-Hellweg, Martin Butler, Lia Chang, Robert Mizono, Kallan Nishimoto, Kumiko Tanaka, Raymond Yuen.

In memory of Herbie Koga . . .

H.V.

Introduction
THE HEARTBEAT OF JAPAN

The Japanese word *taiko* 太鼓 literally means "fat drum." The same word *taiko* is also used to refer to the art of Japanese drumming. Anyone can bang a drum, but that is not really taiko. True taiko is a Way, a spiritual pursuit. When taiko is done correctly, it includes the whole body, the focus of mind and spirit. When I am enjoying the exciting sound of the taiko, I am not just hearing it. I am seeing the beautiful movement of the performers. And I am feeling the power of the drum in my being. It has been said of taiko that "rhythm and joy ride together on the end of a drumstick. Its closest cousin may be gospel singing."

When you put your hand on your chest, you feel the beat of your own heart. Did you know that the heartbeat of your own mother is the very first drum sound you hear? That is why the drum is considered the first instrument in every culture throughout the world. The taiko is the heartbeat of Japan.

The Way of Taiko is over a thousand years old, and its development has taken many paths in Japan. The taiko drum makes so powerful a sound that in ancient times it was said the boundaries of a Japanese village were determined by how far the sound of the village drum would carry.

The taiko symbolized community, not just as a musical instrument in public performance but as a basic means of communication within a village. Most villages had at least one drum, and its various rhythms were used for all aspects of everyday life. The drum was used to gather townspeople or warn of danger. It was beaten to signal war and send samurai into battle. Drummed messages could be sent across great distances in the village. Farmers would take the drums to the fields and drive pests from the crops or awaken the spirit of rain. Many villages had songs that were uniquely their own, so the rhythm of the beats would have great meaning. In some fishing villages, for example, when the fishermen went out to sea, the people who stayed behind would play the drum in the evening so the fishermen would know which village to come home to.

Entire villages would celebrate with festivals accompanied by drum music. Harvest celebrations, festivals signifying seasonal changes, festivals in honor of one's ancestors, New Year's celebrations: all these have a taiko component. The sound of the drum is said to call the gods to Earth to celebrate.

The Japanese emperor has for centuries included taiko in special imperial court music that speaks directly to the spirits; even today the imperial household employs drum makers who have carried on the secrets of the taiko for generations. The techniques of drum making are closely held. A master craftsman may only pass his skills on to a chosen successor.

Taiko plays a key rhythmic role in ensembles that accompany performances of traditional Japanese theater (such as Noh); during Kabuki plays the drum also creates sound effects to represent various natural elements—like rain and thunder—that occur in the story.

Today, taiko continues to be used in all the traditional venues, in religious ceremonies, festivals, classical theaters, and ancestor worship. It is estimated that there are more than 5,000 taiko groups in Japan, and nearly 200 in the United States. Some are professional taiko ensembles, with full-time taiko performers. By and large, however, most taiko players have regular jobs and study and appreciate the art form during their leisure hours. Even as a weekend or evening activity, playing the drum, hearing the drum, and feeling its resonance are healthy components of our modern lives. The drum returns us to the time of our ancestors, a time when we were bodies dancing on hillsides, not a pair of eyes staring at a TV or computer screen.

This book is only an introduction to the Way of Taiko and is organized into three main sections: A Brief History of Taiko, Understanding Sounds and Movements, and Training in the Way. It is for audiences who are curious about taiko or who are looking to more fully appreciate taiko performances. It is also for people already doing taiko, to deepen their understanding of the art. The need for information in English, even among the taiko community, is great. It is my hope that this book will provide a useful tool to those seeking answers. Finally, *The Way of Taiko* is for those of you who may be inspired to begin learning taiko, to encourage you to take the next step in your journey. You do not learn an instrument to play it; you play it to learn.

A Brief History of Taiko

The Goddess and the Drum

One day, Amaterasu, the Sun Goddess, was so angered by the teasing of her brother, Susano-wo, the Thunder God, that she locked herself in a cave, rolled a huge stone across the entrance, and vowed never to come out again. The world lay in darkness. The other gods pleaded and threatened and brought in priests and magicians and mighty warriors to roll back the stone, but to no avail. All knew that if the Sun Goddess kept her light hidden in the cave too long, the plants and the animals of the world would surely die. At last, Uzume, a wild and wily goddess, announced that she could lure Amaterasu from the cave. The others sneered. Uzume simply smiled as she opened a sake barrel and turned it upside down. Then she began the most boisterous beating upon the head and frenetic dancing that any had ever seen or heard. All around her laughed and rejoiced as she danced and pounded on the barrel. Amaterasu, hearing the commotion, wondered what could so amuse the gods to cause them to forget the darkness. Stepping closer to the stone blocking the cave's entrance, she could feel the rhythms pulsing through the stone and through her body. Curious, the Sun Goddess rolled away the stone and joined the others in the festivities. And that is how sunlight returned to the world and how the first taiko was made.

—based on a retelling by Stan Shikuma
of a traditional Japanese tale

Drums in Ancient Asia and Japan

The exact history of Japanese taiko is unclear. Daihachi Oguchi of the Osuwa Daiko troupe in Nagano Prefecture suggests that taiko-style drums may have been used as early as Japan's prehistoric Jomon period, some 4,000 years ago. While it is possible that taiko drums originated in Japan, the use of drums throughout human history and the similarity of modern Japanese taiko to instruments in China, Korea, India, and Mesopotamia suggests cultural influence from the Silk Road. A relief from a Sumerian castle dated 3000–2000 BCE depicts a person playing a drum some 6 feet in diameter that is similar to a taiko. Instruments similar to drums like the *doumbek* (a ceramic-bodied hand drum from the Middle East) have been unearthed in Japan from as far back as 2500 BCE.

Waves of cultural influence from Korea and China appeared in Japan from 300 to 900 CE, during the Yamato, Nara, and early Heian periods. The oldest surviving physical artifact of a taiko is a *haniwa* (small clay burial figurine) from the 6th century depicting a man with a drum covered in skins on both sides and hung from his shoulder at hip height. He is playing it with a stick in his right hand; the left hand is empty. Similarities between this style of playing and those in China and Korea reinforce the theory of a Silk Road influence.

Traditional Japanese Music

Kagura: Sacred Music

Japan's indigenous form of worship is known as Shinto, the Way of the Gods. One of Japan's earliest forms of sacred music is Kagura. Whether it is performed in the formal precincts of the Imperial Palace in Tokyo or in some small village shrine, Kagura—combining song, dance, and the beats of a single drum—always signifies a performance intended as an offering and an entertainment to the ancient gods. The word Kagura means "place of the gods" but is written with the characters 神楽, "music of the gods."

In old Japan, as in many early cultures, the drum was an intimate part of many village activities. Simple beats might be used when hunters set out, at the coming of a storm, or when calling fishermen back from the sea. The thankful people began to believe each drum to be inhabited by the divine. The drum from each village was thus thought to protect the inhabitants. Played at harvests and festivals, the drum would imitate the sound of thunder and encourage the spirit of rain into action, or scare away evil demons that might threaten the village's well-being.

The taiko has thus always had associations with spirituality. There are written references to taiko in the creation myth of the goddess Amaterasu, first written down in the 8th century. The drum is created exclusively with natural elements and is considered in one sense to be a living thing. Its round shape represents an unbroken line. In some religious sects, the drum was considered the voice of the Buddha. The *uchiwa-daiko*, or "fan drum"—frequently seen in taiko performances today—was developed by the Nichiren sect of Buddhism to accompany their chants.

In villages, because the drum was used in prayers to please the *kami* (gods) in hopes of good harvests for farmers or good catches for fishermen, the tradition developed that only holy men were allowed to beat the taiko drum. It is believed that the taiko not only heralds the spirits, but that spirits inhabit the drum. Taiko performances today sometimes begin with invocations or prayers to the gods.

Gagaku: Taiko in the Imperial Court

As a result of foreign influence and the development of native culture, various drums and musical ensemble styles emerged in Japan during the Nara and Heian periods (700–1185). The direct predecessor of the modern hanging-frame taiko is believed to have come across the Eurasian continent to Japan with Buddhism around the

7th century. Gigaku was a masked drama with singers, flutes, and drums. Rinyugaku was music based on Southeast Asia pantomimes.

What evolved into the traditional court music of Japan is known as Gagaku. Gagaku is an elite and esoteric music performed with dance and pantomime. It flourished during the Heian period, when it was the near-exclusive pursuit of nobles and aristocrats, who used it primarily for ceremonial occasions in the Imperial Palace. It took various forms. Togaku was an ensemble style derived from T'ang China. Komagaku came from the three Korean kingdoms and was played in a smaller ensemble.

Little changed since the 11th century, Gagaku is still played by ensembles of winds, strings, and percussion. While the central element in Gagaku is the wind section (distinguished by the eerie, reedy sound of the *sho*, or mouth organ), the *tsuzumi* (hand drum) plays a dynamic percussive role. Other drum or drumlike instruments seen in Gagaku are the cylin-

der-shaped drum (*kakko*), the bronze gong (*shoko*), and a large, ornate hanging drum (*taiko*) struck by two heavy drumsticks. Modern taiko performances include these and many other types of drum.

No notations from this early period exist, but it is clear that taiko were used in all of these types of music. For example, one literary reference from the Heian period depicts a performance of Gigaku with a rendering of a *suri-tsuzumi*, a type of Japanese hanging drum similar to drums that originated during China's T'ang dynasty and, in earlier times, India. A mural depicting Bugaku (imperial court dance) features a musician holding a drum on his lap with his left hand and playing with his right.

After the year 900, wholesale importation of culture from China tapered off and Japanese music developed primarily under native influence. Over time, taiko developed independent styles that had to do with the varied structure of Japan's strict class-based society. There are thus various paths that have led taiko to where it is today.

Taiko in Noh and Kabuki

Taiko ensembles associated with Japanese traditional theater are highly stylized and regimented, and the musicians who perform in them are classically trained in one of several schools (*ryuha*). Some forms of traditional theater in Japan use music ensembles to comment on the action on stage, somewhat like a soundtrack for a movie. Smaller taiko are usually a part of theatrical ensembles, but these are played very differently from taiko that are used at festivals or at a modern taiko performance.

There began to form, toward the end of the Heian period, provincial ensembles that included taiko as part of the instrumentation. Created by musicians and minstrels who attached themselves to temples and shrines, these early ensembles performed music and mime for the plebian class. Dengaku, or "field music," was a combination of music and dance associated with rice cultivation. Sarugaku, or "monkey music," was a somewhat more developed entertainment that included many comic elements.

In the Muromachi period (1335–1573), Kyotsugu Kannami and his son, Motokyo Zeami, inspired by Chinese theater, combined sacred chanting and well-known verses with the popular music and dance conventions of Dengaku and Sarugaku to create Noh theater. Noh incorporates dance-drama, chorus, and music and features distinctive costumes, masks, and scenery. While the performance is austere, Noh uses heroic themes that center around humans, gods, and demons.

Nogaku is the music of Noh theater. The instrumental ensemble (*no hayashi*) consists of three drums and a flute: the *shime-daiko* (on a low stand with skins perpendicular to the floor, used only in the dance segments), the *ko-tsuzumi* (a small hourglass-shaped drum that rests on the musician's shoulder and is played by hand), the *o-tsuzumi* (a larger version that rests on the player's left hip), and the *nokan* (a six-holed, transverse, high-pitched bamboo flute). An important part of the music in Noh consists of vocalizations—pitched calls—that add to the musical rhythm and to the drama of the performance.

Kabuki is a colorful costumed theater that developed in the 17th century (Edo period) for the common people, who enjoyed its themes based on historical events, moral conflicts, and love relationships. Kabuki features an all-male cast of actors playing highly stylized female roles, and has drawn its influences from classical dance, elements of Noh, and elsewhere. The music of Kabuki is similarly of a mixed tradition and consists of a drum and flute ensemble accompanying song and *shamisen* (a banjolike instrument). *Geza ongaku* ("offstage music") from an ensemble of musicians hidden from the audience provides sound effects (like thunder or rain) or elaborates on the action; for example, the slow beat of a taiko here may hint at an impending tragedy, or the pluck of a koto may create an air of refinement.

Festival and Folk Music

Displaying its religious roots, taiko contin-

The taiko family tree.

ues to have an important role in festivals throughout Japan, calling the *kami* to be a part of the celebrations. Taiko is always a part of Obon ceremonies in the hot summer that honor one's ancestors with song and community dancing. The drums are played at harvest festivals to give thanks to the *kami* (for a bountiful crop) and are used during Oshogatsu (New Year's) festivals to bring good luck for the coming year. Some of the techniques of taiko drumming are thought to be based on the motions made by rice farmers as they swing their arms to harvest the crop. As a regular accompaniment to *minyo* (Japanese folk music), taiko was popular with farmers, peasants, and the merchant class.

Japan's festival tradition has followed the movements of Japanese emigrants. The most well-known festivals in America are the Sakura Matsuri (Spring Cherry Blossom) celebrations held in Japantowns and at churches and community centers wherever there is a sizable Japanese American population. These days, taiko performances are a regular feature of the ceremonies and entertainments.

Some established taiko festival pieces are associated in Japan with a particular city, region, or Buddhist temple or Shinto shrine. Many older folk pieces are maintained by a kind of taiko group known as a *hozonkai* (preservation society), whose mission is to carry ancient taiko traditions to the modern day. *Hozonkai* are cultural custodians; they look after the performance details and assure their authenticity. They also grant permission to other groups who seek to perform established pieces, as taiko ensembles try to respect each other's works and traditions. An example of a taiko *hozonkai* is Gojinjo Daiko, which is dedicated to preserving the centuries-old taiko tradition of the village of Nafune on the Japan Sea.

Drums at War

The sound of the drum, depending on the size and skill of the player, can carry two miles and may have demarcated the village boundaries. This range of sound made taiko useful on the battlefield. Like drums in many cultures, taiko in Japan were used to intimidate the enemy and, by the 14th century, to issue commands and coordinate troop movements. Images on picture scrolls and screens depict soldiers carrying both long-bodied and rope-tensioned drums lashed to their backs, with one or two other soldiers beating out rhythms on them. The Osuwa Daiko museum in Nagano Prefecture has a war drum that belonged to the great feudal lord Takara Shingen. Taiko are still used in the dojo (training halls) of various martial arts worldwide.

Ensemble Drumming

After its centuries-long history in Japan as a solo or accompanying instrument, taiko in modern times has found its most popular role as the lead instrument in the *kumidaiko,* the taiko ensemble. In the late 19th and early 20th centuries, westernization— the industrial revolution coupled with the modernization of Japan's institutions— caused the decline of many traditional Japanese folk arts and customs. In the 1930s, a period of economic depression and military aggression further undermined the arts. After World War II, a series of reforms

and restrictions shocked an already exhausted nation. The Japanese felt the need to revive a sense of national identity with a reawakening of traditional values. Taiko was about to be "rediscovered" and changed forever.

Daihachi Oguchi.

A young jazz aficionado named Daihachi Oguchi had been drafted and taken prisoner in China during the war. He returned to his home in Suwa City, Nagano Prefecture, in 1947 and became a drummer in a local jazz band. One day, a relative came across a document in a soybean warehouse that he thought might be a taiko score and brought it to the young drummer to decipher. Oguchi decided to learn the piece and to perform it at the local Suwa Shrine. But, envisioning the traditional solo score as a larger ensemble work, he added new rhythms that he then divided into simple patterns, assigning a role to each musical voice. He devised jazz kits of traditional instruments, using the big *o-daiko* as a kick-drum pulse, the smaller *shime-daiko* to carry the background rhythm, and the medium-size *nagado-daiko* for the melody. The group he formed then began to create their own drums and invent new instruments, like the three-toned bell *tetto* (also referred to as a "cannon"). By 1951, thirty-year-old Daihachi Oguchi had become the leader of the four-hundred-year-old Osuwa Daiko group. Oguchi has since been credited as creator of the kumi-daiko style of performance. Small groups that in olden times had assembled only at festival time to play local music in celebration were about to move onto the world stage.

Taiko in Modern Japan

Across Japan, thanks in part to the new medium of television, the new style of taiko was an instant success, and many groups were formed. The Hokuriku Odaiko Enthusiasts Association and Hokuriku Taiko Association, for example, were established in 1957 and 1958. In 1959, Yoshihisa Ishikura, Yutaka Ishizuka (whose *natori*, or professional name, was Saburo Mochizuki), Seido Kobayashi, and Motoei Onozato (Kiyonari Tosha) founded Yushima Tenjin Sukeroku Daiko—named for the Yushima Tenjin Shrine in Tokyo—playing Edo-bayashi taiko (a style dating back to premodern Tokyo). The group created a dynamic performance style emphasizing speed, fluidity, and power. They incorporated choreography and dance movements and invented special *dai* (drum stands) to facilitate their vision. (The founders eventually went their separate ways. Seido Kobayashi founded the Oedo Sukeroku Daiko, credited as the first fully professional group in the world. Kiyonari Tosha began Nihon Taiko Dojo.)

In 1964, the Olympic Games were held in Tokyo. During the "Festival of the Arts" presentation, Noh, Kabuki, and the "new" taiko groups, among them Osuwa Daiko, were showcased as part of Japan's rediscovery of its national identity. This exposure led to requests from around the country for Daihachi Oguchi to come and teach taiko. Many rural areas formed taiko groups and looked to Oguchi's instruction as a means of revitalizing their villages: not only would an active taiko group give young people a reason not to leave for the city, but it would attract visitors and commerce. Due to his contributions to the art form, the Japanese government officially recognized Grandmaster Daihachi Oguchi as an Intangible Cultural Property. Eventually, Oguchi went on to found groups in Canada, France, Singapore, Indonesia, and the United States (Chicago and St. Louis).

While community groups were being formed and *hozonkai* of ancient regional taiko music established, a completely new kind of taiko group was emerging. In 1969, Tagayasu Den collected a group of youths entirely dedicated to a taiko way of life, and on Sado Island, off the west central coast of Japan, he founded the Za Ondekoza troupe. Rigorous training, daily marathon running, and communal living created taiko performances that awed the world. Za Ondekoza became the first Japanese taiko group to tour the United States in 1977.

In 1981, the original members of Za Ondekoza split with Den, who continued to tour—his powerful drummers running marathons from performance to performance around the United States—until he passed away in 1995. The splinter group remained on Sado Island to form Kodo. They embraced the tradition, sharing a communal lifestyle, practicing rigorously, and running marathons. Kodo has since gained international fame and been a great and driving force in the growth of taiko, its name synonymous to the uninitiated with the art form itself. Kodo has renewed and popularized taiko with its relentless touring, conducting workshops the world over and holding an international percussion festival at its home base. The group spends four months of each year on Sado Island, four months touring Japan, and four months touring abroad.

Part of the growth of taiko in Japan can be traced to a 1975 change in Japan's Cultural Artifacts Preservation Law that made festivals, arts, and customs eligible for subsidy. In 1979 the Nihon Taiko Renmei (All-Japan Taiko League) was formed to facilitate receipt of this newly available governmental support. By the 1980s, the central government was providing money for festivals and community promotion. Many domestic and international taiko tours continue to benefit from government funding.

Taiko in America

The First Wave

Taiko came to America with Japanese immigration in the late 19th and early 20th centuries. America's first documented taiko drum—a large *o-daiko* drum—arrived in San Francisco in 1910. The drum was an important reminder of the culture that had been left behind. As a result of the U.S. Government's forced internment of Japanese during World War II, 110,000 Japanese Americans lost their land, their belongings and, in some cases, their ties to any family back in Japan. Following their release from the camps, many downplayed their culture and language for fear of reprisal and assimilated into the American culture. Japanese community traditions and cultural expression took a heavy loss.

The taiko that had arrived in 1910 languished silent in a warehouse.

In 1967, twenty-four-year-old Seiichi Tanaka from Nagano Prefecture attended the annual Cherry Blossom Festival in San Francisco. It was unlike any such festival in Japan. In Japan, the taiko were a part of almost every festival, to bring good luck and good fortune, to invite the gods to participate. But in San Francisco, there were no taiko to call the *kami*, to bring good luck, to accompany any dance. The only taiko in America, in fact, were single instruments stored away in Buddhist temples and used to accompany Bon Festival dancing in late summer.

The next year, in 1968, with borrowed instruments, Tanaka was the sole drummer at the San Francisco Cherry Blossom Festival. That same year he founded the San Francisco Taiko Dojo, the first kumi-daiko ensemble in the United States. In 1969, the dynamic Sukeroku Taiko of Tokyo performed at the Circle Star Theater in Redwood City, California. There, Tanaka was able to meet the artists and forge a bond that has lasted more than thirty-five years and, in many ways, determined the style of taiko in America.

Seiichi Tanaka pioneered the art of taiko in the United States—forged by the training of Daihachi Oguchi from his own Nagano Prefecture, supported by Sukeroku Taiko and *hozonkai* like Gojinjo Daiko, and influenced by his own martial arts training as well as the sounds and rhythms of Western music. When the forgotten *o-daiko* was discovered in a Japan Airlines warehouse

in San Francisco, it was given to Tanaka in recognition of his leadership (at the time, it was the largest such drum in America). Since then, Tanaka has continued to bring taiko to varied audiences through appearances in films like *Rising Sun* and in

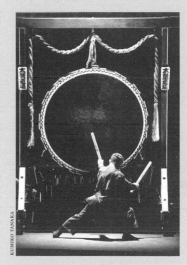

Grandmaster Seiichi Tanaka.

concerts with jazz, Latin, and African musicians and percussionists. The San Francisco Taiko Dojo also produces an annual International Taiko Festival. With the formation in 1993 of the Nihon Taiko Dojo, the first school in Japan based on the teachings of Seiichi Tanaka, American taiko is now in the position of exporting taiko *back* to Japan. To date, Tanaka estimates he has trained some 10,000 students. He is also the only taiko artist to receive the esteemed

NEA National Heritage Fellowship for his contribution to traditional arts.

In those early years, American taiko was still finding its voice. Demand was growing, and new American groups were springing up, practicing on car tires to save the precious few drums available for performances.

Masao Kodani is the minister of the Senshin Buddhist Temple in Los Angeles. After the 1969 Obon Festival, he and fellow temple member George Abe formed Kinnara Taiko, the first contemporary taiko group to come directly from the Japanese American community. Named after the celestial musicians of Buddhism, Kinnara Taiko was the first kumi-daiko group to be associated with a Buddhist tradition. As Japanese ensembles are generally associated with Shinto, this type of drumming has no direct ancestor in Japan. Technically, Kinnara Taiko considers itself neither Japanese taiko nor American drumming but "mass drumming outside of a ritual context to teach Buddhist ideals."

The prohibitive cost and unavailability of Japanese drums put the two new American groups, San Francisco Taiko Dojo and Kinnara Taiko, at a disadvantage compared to the flourishing kumi-daiko groups in Japan. A quality, medium-size drum might cost $6,000. Kinnara Taiko's innovation of making long-bodied drums (*nagado-daiko*) from oak wine barrels was one impetus for the subsequent wild growth of American taiko groups. Having relatively affordable drums made it possible for emerging performers to practice, develop their skills, and showcase their work. Member Johnny Mori, for example, helped raise awareness of the art outside of the Japanese communities through his performances in the jazz ensemble Hiroshima.

PJ and Roy Hirabayashi formed San Jose Taiko to express the beauty and harmony of the human spirit through the voice of the taiko. Since 1973, the troupe has toured the world and founded and supported developing ensembles throughout the United States and Canada. They embellish their traditional rhythms of Japanese drumming with world rhythms including African, Balinese, Latin, and Jazz percussion. San Jose remains one of the most active and well-known taiko ensembles in the United States, touring, conducting workshops, offering classes, and consulting on the future of the art by creating conferences and dialogues. San Jose Taiko's greatest innovations are their extraordinary collaborations with artists and companies from various disciplines to create new and vibrant productions and inspire growth in the art of Japanese American taiko. In 2003, they brought all three First Wave groups together for historic performances in each community to celebrate the last three Japantowns left in America.

The Second Wave

After Kenny Endo saw a San Francisco Taiko Dojo performance in 1973 he determined to someday study the art. He joined Kinnara Taiko in 1975, and after graduating from college moved to San Francisco, where he studied with Seiichi Tanaka from 1976 to 1980, supporting himself playing drum kit in clubs at night. Endo made the choice between drum kit and taiko and, with Sensei Tanaka's introductions to Daihachi Oguchi, Osuwa Daiko, and Sukeroku Daiko, went to Japan to study. He spent a decade in Japan, performing professionally and studying kumi-daiko and traditional Japanese music. He became the only non-Japanese national to receive a *natori* (stage name) and thus is now officially recognized as a teacher in the Mochizuki school of Hogaku Hayashi, a classical style of flute and drum performance for the Kabuki theater. Through the Taiko Center of the Pacific, based in Honolulu, Endo leads a rigorous schedule of teaching and performance. Because of his cross-cultural studies, he is in a unique position in the world of taiko. His experimentation may very well lead to the next level of the art.

Shasta Taiko in northern California was formed in 1985 by Jeanne Mercer and

Russel Baba, who moved from San Francisco Taiko Dojo to begin a unique ensemble. One of its members, Mark Miyoshi, has become the first American to focus on and advance the building of stave (that is, barrel construction) taiko, which have become the mainstay of many American taiko ensembles. His innovations have led to significant improvements in the drum. Meanwhile, the excellent training and performance of Mercer and Baba have inspired their son Masato to become one of the leaders of a new generation of taiko artists.

Soh Daiko in New York, founded in 1979, did not have the luxury of developing on the West Coast where all the taiko "action" was brewing. As leaders of the first taiko group in the eastern U.S., Alan and Merle Okada made it their mission to study the history of taiko and thus built their group piece by piece, learning as they grew. Today, Soh Daiko is one of the finest troupes in North America.

Other important Second Wave groups include Denver Taiko, Seattle Kokon Taiko, Los Angeles Matsuri Taiko, and Katari Taiko (in Vancouver, B.C., the first Canadian taiko group).

New Voices

There are many more stories from around the nation. There are taiko groups that formed after they found a drum hidden away. There are groups that started when someone was inspired by a performance of one of the First or Second Wave American kumi-daiko ensembles. There are groups created out of nostalgia for festivals in Japan or as a powerful way to assert their identity as Japanese Americans. Whatever the reason, a Third and a Fourth wave of kumi-daiko in America have already emerged, and surely more will follow.

Taiko is also moving in new and exciting directions. No longer is a taiko displayed only at festivals or at kumi-daiko performances. Jazz ensembles like Hiroshima (with Johnny Mori on taiko) and other performers like Kitaro incorporate the drum into their performances. Elaborate theater pieces use taiko as entertainment and for social commentary. There are women's taiko groups, children's groups, senior ensembles, and community and religious groups. Taiko is even used in drum circles and corporate team-building workshops.

Taiko as music therapy has been serving special populations for decades. Teachers have learned to present taiko to develop empathy, intimacy, structure, and redirection. Taiko is used in mental health facilities and prisons, and there are at-risk youth programs as well as deaf and disabled performers. There is true healing in being able to beat the drum. To join with others and communicate without words is empowering, creating a bonding and sharing that is both subliminal and kinesthetic. Taiko players create expression and also react to one another. It is likely this special bond that is the impetus for the phenomenal growth of the art form today.

The Future of Taiko

The founding of the First Wave groups—San Francisco Taiko Dojo, Kinnara Taiko, and San Jose Taiko—occurred at a time of great social upheaval in America. The Japanese American groups were influenced by civil rights, the budding Asian American movement, and a shared history of repression. Japanese national Seiichi Tanaka had a very different background and sensibility.

These distinctive characteristics in the pioneers of American taiko and their early and profound influences on the development of the art are what make American taiko different from Japanese taiko. American taiko is now a unique art form, incorporating the traditions of Japan with the melting-pot influences of the New World.

The future of taiko now depends on the members of the taiko community. The great joy of sharing a powerful and special art has led to incredible connections worldwide. With innovations and collaborations from groups both new and established, the future is bright for creativity and continued growth. Hundreds of groups have formed, in America and around the world, thousands in Japan.

But dissemination of the art has led to some diluting of core values. For example, leaders from San Francisco Taiko Dojo, San Jose Taiko, and Kodo in Japan all lament how new groups appropriate their original material and fail to recognize its origins. Many younger groups do not ask permission or follow accepted etiquette between community members. Although some may feel that the *hozonkai* in Japan are too restrictive in their efforts to protect traditional pieces from unauthorized use, they are generally quite willing to teach and share what they know. The situation in Japan is influenced by long-established relationships and traditions. In America, communication and understanding will have to be the key.

Classical Japanese music (and other Japanese traditional arts) are held to rigorous standards and forms. Most taiko as it is exhibited in America has its roots in the fairly new ensemble style of kumi-daiko. While taiko should display creativity, it is also important to be true to the unique character of the art. You cannot deviate too far and still be relevant. Expansive growth has led many inexperienced taiko practitioners to instruct prematurely, causing unnecessary injury to curious beginners and sometimes presenting the art too many generations removed from its roots.

True taiko is not only the *omote* (appearance), but also the *ura* (that which is inside). Groups and individuals will have to hold themselves to standards of personal, artistic, and professional integrity to further taiko as a viable art. It is up to the taiko community to define what taiko is and what it will become. Let us hope that the leaders of today and the leaders of tomorrow set the standards high and strive for a dynamic future.

San Jose Taiko.

Kodo.

Kodo.

San Francisco Taiko Dojo featuring Koichi Tamano.

San Francisco Taiko Dojo.

FRANCISCO VILLAFLOR

Kinnara Taiko.

Kinnara Taiko.

San Jose Taiko.

Kenny Endo on o-daiko.

LIA CHANG

Endo on taiko set.

Ume Taiko Dan, Penryn, California.

Understanding Sounds and Movements

THE LION DANCE

Mukashi, mukashi . . . long, long ago there was no television and no radio, and knowledge of books belonged to the scholars and the monks. But the people traveled and traded and shared their stories in journeys that lasted generations. The world's oldest trade route is the Silk Road; people traveled it back and forth, from North Africa, through Mesopotamia, and across the Asian continent. And when they reached Japan, along with them came the stories of a powerful and magical creature. Taiko and flute accompany the dance of this animal, who brings good luck and good fortune. This is the Shi

Shi Mai, the Japanese lion dance. One dancer wears the proud hand-carved mask of the golden female or of the great red male, with a mane of flowing horse-hair. You see, Japan being an island, no one had ever seen this magnificent creature, and had only heard the stories that grew and changed over the centuries. Today, the Shi Shi Mai dance is still performed in Japan, particularly at New Year's, to bestow good luck to all. If the Shi Shi Mai lion bites you, it is especially good luck. The creature is a great benefactor, and it is still believed that if you feed the lion money, wealth will find you.

Taiko: Japanese Drums

The modern art of kumi-daiko—the taiko ensemble—is continually evolving and variously draws on all of the traditional styles of Japanese music. One way the art differs from its original incarnation is that modern kumi-daiko ensembles frequently play several taiko styles, and not just regional specialties. In this way, the groups draw on standard instrumentation while adding other elements. This section offers a brief introduction to a few of the types of drums you might see used in a taiko performance.

Taiko are hand-made by artisans who have developed their traditions over generations. Until recently, with the advent of the Internet, creation of these instruments was a closely guarded secret among families and companies. One company, Miyamoto Unosuke Shoten of Tokyo, has been the official drum maker to the emperor for generations. The discussion of instruments in this section in general describes them as they have been traditionally made in Japan. Modern instruments, especially those made outside of Japan, may be produced with different materials and manufacturing methods.

Generally speaking, there are only two types of taiko, and both have skins on two sides of the drum.

Byo-daiko

The body of the *byo-daiko* is carved from a single log. The heads of the drum are specially tuned by a master craftsman and then nailed into place. The drum cannot then be tuned without removing the heads.

The drum heads are generally made from the hide of three-to-four-year-old black Holstein cows or, for larger instruments, Holstein bulls. The treatment of the hides and the subsequent creation of the heads is part of what distinguishes one master drum maker from another. The skins of these drums are thick compared with those of many types of drums around the world, as the players are meant to strike

Chu-daiko (josuke).

O-daiko.

them with drumsticks and with considerable force.

The favored wood for the body of the taiko is zelkova (known in Japan as *keyaki*, a relative of the elm). Other woods such as horse chestnut and camphor are used on less-expensive drums, and the largest drums are often carved from *bubinga* (from Africa).

In olden days, each drum was hand-carved from a single tree trunk that was allowed to dry for several years using a generations-old "secret" technique that kept the wood from splitting as it dried out. A master carpenter would then chisel out the drum body by hand from the hard and beautifully grained zelkova. The particular texture left on the inside of the wood would mellow the tone when the drum was struck. Today, the instruments are shaped on a massive lathe. A large log can yield a great drum; the hollowed-out inside can be formed into a smaller instrument, and so on.

Large shime-daiko.

Hira-daiko.

There are two types of byo-daiko. The *nagado-daiko* (also referred to as the *miya-daiko* or temple drum) is a long-bodied drum and is frequently seen at festivals, temples, and shrines. Different types of nagado-daiko are often referred to by their size, although a "standard" size would be 18 inches across and 22 inches high. *Ko-daiko* (also called *sumo*), for example, means "small drum." *Chu-daiko*—the name means "medium-size drum" (it is referred to as *josuke* or *jozuke* when it sits on a slanted stand)—is the most common type of taiko, used frequently in kumi-daiko, where it usually carries the melody. It generally weighs about 60 pounds.

The largest nagado-daiko is known as an *o-daiko*, literally "big, fat drum." The term is usually reserved for drums with a head 3 feet to 6 feet in diameter or more. An o-daiko is the most dynamic of the taiko instruments and is usually played horizontally—skins perpendicular to the floor—by one to two performers. Nagado-

Rope-tightened (L) and bolt-tightened tsukeshime-daiko (R).

Oke-daiko on angled stand.

daiko have a deep, reverberant sound. In live performance, the o-daiko is the drum with sounds so deep that the music is felt in the body as well as heard. Because of its dominant power, this type of drum is what people imagine when they think of taiko.

The *hira-daiko* is a shallow-bodied drum. It can be a small instrument or an o-daiko-size creation that weighs many tons. The tone of the drum is deep and reverberant with a short decay. It is also used as an orchestral instrument in classical Kabuki and dance music.

Shime-daiko

The *shime-daiko* is a rope-tensioned drum. The word *shime* comes from the Japanese verb *shimeru*, which means to bind or tighten up. Strictly speaking, the term *shime-daiko* is applied to a small drum used in classical Japanese music, such as that performed with Noh and Kabuki. The body is one piece of hardwood, typically *keyaki*, which is often lacquered and beautifully decorated. Hides are stretched over steel rings and the skin is sewn tightly to itself by a skilled craftsman. A seamstress stitches around the ring and trims the original sewing. A skin is then placed on either side

Ko-tsuzumi.

O-tsuzumi.

of the prepared drum body and tensioned to holes in each skin with rope. The skin is thinner than on a nagado-daiko and the tone is higher pitched, rather like a snare drum. Occasionally the edges are painted with gold, and in the middle of the head is a circular patch of deer skin.

The heavier version of this drum, with thicker skins and a stronger body, is properly called a *tsukeshime-daiko* and is used as a basic beat or solo instrument in ensemble playing and folk music.

In modern versions of both small and large shime-daiko, the heads are sometimes attached with bolt assembly instead of being tied with rope. These drums must be tightened and tuned before the performance and loosened afterward.

The *oke-daiko*, commonly called *oke-do*, is a rope-tensioned drum that has a body made with stave construction (like a wine barrel, whose importance in modern American taiko was mentioned earlier). The heads of the instrument are designed the same as on a smaller shime-daiko, but the size of the drum itself can vary, from a sling drum that the performer can carry to an instrument with heads more than 10 feet high. The only limit to the size of an okedo is the size of the skins. The sound of the instrument varies widely according to its size.

The *ko-tsuzumi* is a hand-held instrument similar to the African talking drum. Shaped like an hourglass, the body is lacquered and decorated. The drum is held on the right shoulder and played with the right hand. The player controls the sound

Bachi.

Uchiwa-
daiko.

Atarigane.

by squeezing and releasing—that is, adjusting the tension of—the ropes with the left hand. The pitch of the ko-tsuzumi is very high, with a short decay. The drum is often used in theater for accent; the drummer's *kakegoe*—stylized vocalizations that can sound like deep-throated yelps—are a part of the performance. The heads are made of deer skin and are removed after each use. The ko-tsuzumi is used in Japanese classical music, and any musician who plays it on stage must have received a special rank (known as *natori*). The *o-tsuzumi* is a larger version of the ko-tsuzumi and rests on the player's left hip. It is sometimes played with finger caps called *saku*.

Drumsticks

There are as many types of drumsticks—collectively known as *bachi*—as there are varieties of taiko. Most taiko are played with sticks with a few exceptions, like the ko-tsuzumi, which is played with the hand. Bachi are generally made of white oak, Japanese magnolia, cypress, or bamboo. In a taiko ensemble, players generally prefer to use their own bachi and never pick up someone else's sticks without permission.

When players want to increase volume, they raise the drumsticks as high as their field of peripheral vision when looking toward the audience. In Japanese theater, different effects are created by using special drumsticks (such as those of bamboo) or by varying the angle of the attack. It is said that a traditional nagado-daiko can make up to seven different sounds; there are special beats that represent "soundtrack"

Tetsu-zutsu (tetto).

Chappa.

elements like thunder or raindrops, or feelings of apprehension.

Narimono (Percussion)

Various rattles, shakers, and other noise-makers are known collectively as *narimono*. Festival music uses these instruments to accompany the taiko, while traditional Japanese theater uses them to produce sound effects.

Developed by a Buddhist sect to aid in chanting is the *uchiwa-daiko* or fan drum. It is held in one hand and played with one stick. Fan drums can be as small as a ping-pong paddle or nearly 3 feet across. The drum makes a percussive burst, and movement of the hand holding the drum gives a vibrato sound to the decay.

The *atarigane* (or *kane*) is a brass hand-held, bell-like instrument that comes in different sizes and tones and is played with a deer antler ringer. It is used to keep time in taiko festival ensemble music and as an accent. The *tetsu-zutsu* or *tetto* (known in America as a "cannon") is a relatively new instrument developed by the Osuwa Daiko group. It sits on a stand and consists of three sizes of pipe welded together to simulate the sound of the atarigane. Some groups keep time using sections of bamboo played with sticks.

Chappa (small cymbals) originated in

Shoko.

Sasara.

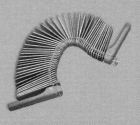

Tibetan singing bowls, a reflection of the Buddhist aspect of the art, are used in Japanese music as an important counterpoint in serious pieces.

Buddhist temples but are now part of festival music and are played with lively movement and dance. *Shoko* (brass gongs) are often used in Gagaku to build musical dynamics. There is also the wooden instrument known as a *sasara*, which sounds like the rattles of a snake. The sasara consists of 108 oblong blocks of soft wood, tied together in a string. When played, it is considered to represent and dissipate what Buddhists think of as the 108 sins of man.

Instruments from other cultures have also made their way into modern taiko.

Gakki: Instruments

In traditional Japanese theater (such as Kabuki or Noh) or in Japanese court music (such as Gagaku), other instruments are added to the sound of the taiko to create classical music ensembles. Japanese music is based on a quarter-note scale and is too broad a topic for this book. What follows here, then, is a brief introduction to some of the types of instruments you may see at a taiko performance that also features

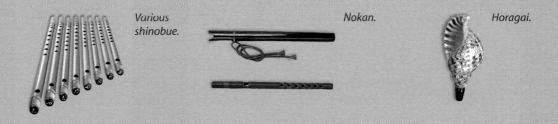

Various shinobue.   *Nokan.*   *Horagai.*

traditional Japanese music and ensemble playing.

Wind Instruments

The *shinobue* is a horizontally played flute made of thin bamboo with seven holes. Different sizes are used to produce different keys. Used in festival music, it is high pitched and can be very evocative. The *nokan* is a six-holed, lacquered horizontal flute used in Noh and Kabuki theater. It is played like the shinobue, but its sound is much more piercing.

A *shakuhachi* is a five-holed, recorder-like flute that is associated with Buddhism. Unlike the shinobue and nokan, the shakuhachi is played vertically and is very breathy and subtle. The shakuhachi is the most difficult flute to play, but its sound is delicate and mesmerizing. The name of the flute refers to its length in *shaku*, a traditional Japanese unit of measure (about 1 foot).

The *horagai* (conchlike shell) sounds like a foghorn and is often used to call to the *kami*.

Among the instruments from older musical forms like Gagaku are the *sho*, a hand-held mouth organ made up of seventeen bamboo pipes arranged in a circle, with a reedy tone evocative of a pipe organ; a double-reed transverse flute called the *hichiriki*; and the *ryuteki*, a seven-holed transverse flute.

Stringed Instruments

Stringed instruments are usually reserved

Sho.

for performances of Japanese traditional music. The *shamisen* (similar to a banjo) is a three-stringed instrument played with a large triangular pick; it is often used in Kabuki but can be a solo instrument. The *koto* (similar to a zither) is a thirteen-stringed instrument that sits low on the floor; the performer sits and plays it with both hands. The *biwa* (similar to a lute) can have three to five strings and offers a bass-like accompaniment.

Kiai and Other Vocalizations

Vocalizations are an important part of any taiko performance, offering invocations, encouragement, timing, and directions to others. These shouts, which precede the beat, are called *kiai* and represent vocalizations of *ki*, known as *chi* in China, an important Asian concept meaning "life energy" or spirit; a kiai is thus a "spirit voice." Kiai can be used as signals of timing among the drummers on stage; sometimes, the drummers call out an actual count, but often kiai serve as the "voice" of their spirit, as an encouragement both to soloists and to each other. Kiai are also voiced to oneself, to help get past a seemingly insurmountable physical boundary in performance. Most of what is shouted out is not words, but random in nature. In classical Japanese music, the kakegoe vocalizations of a ko-tsuzumi player are highly stylized. In Japanese martial arts, the kiai is an art form unto itself; its sound is meant to freeze an enemy in his tracks.

In many Japanese festival songs, the drum is but an accompaniment to the singing. Some well-known songs are sung and played throughout Japan; others are regional in nature. Choral singing and dance are the focus of Noh theater, and the taiko is part of the "orchestra." Taiko can also serve as an aid to the beat or rhythm for chanting in Buddhist and Shinto ceremonies. Sometimes these chants are accompanied by taiko and bells or precede a musical piece at a religious festival.

At the dojo, taiko rhythms and techniques are taught mainly by words called *kuchishoga*, which represent the various sounds of the drums and other instruments. For example, "don" refers to a loud sound played at the center of the head of the nagado-daiko. See the section "Waza" in the next chapter for more on these special vocalizations.

Regalia and Costumes

Calling what taiko performers wear on stage a "costume" is a bit misleading, since that term evokes something you might wear to dress up for a play or at Halloween. Traditional clothing worn in performance and other demonstrations of any culture is not meant to encourage you to become something you are not, but to enhance the performance by accurately representing the art's cultural traditions.

The art of taiko was a part of everyday life before fading into obscurity in the wake of World War II and the suppression of many traditional arts in Japan. With the reawakening of the Way of Taiko in the last few decades in Japan and throughout the world have come professional taiko ensembles. Their regalia (clothing, headbands, insignias, crests, and so on) reflect not only a revival of traditional attire, but the modernization of that attire for the sake of performance. The clothing and regalia on display during a taiko performance vary by geographic region, and since taiko ranges from formal court music to country-style festival drumming, they vary by style of music as well. While performers often wear colored *obi* or belts, these are decorative only and do not indicate any kind of ranking as they do in American martial arts.

Formal Wear

Much of what you might see in a perfor- mance of Gagaku or Noh is as stylized as the art itself. Classical artists prefer the *hakama* of the monk: dark, loose-fitting long pants intended to obscure the foot- work of the martial artist from combatants. Many professional ensembles favor an up- dated version of the attire of the samurai. Imperial court music requires even more elaborate attire (as well as a *natori*—stage name—granted by a teacher when you at- tain a certain level of performance).

In the United States, those not all that familiar with taiko tend to associate it with the group Kodo and men wearing a stark white *fundoshi* (basically a loincloth) in performance. Audiences may also associ- ate the *fundoshi* with what is worn by sumo wrestlers, and this association in fact is not that far off. The *fundoshi* is worn only by performers who have attained a certain level of accomplishment on the o-daiko; it thus represents that individual's commit- ment and at the same time gives spectators the chance to appreciate the performer's physical and mental achievements.

Festival Wear

Many festival drum groups wear the cloth- ing once traditionally worn by Japanese carpenters and workmen to symbolize how their music is accessible to Everyman. This would normally include *tabi* (split-toed, soft-topped outdoor shoes), *momohiki* (ta- pered pants that wrap around and tie at the front and back), and *donburi* (a carpenter's apron).

Performers may also add a *happi* coat, a short jacket emblazoned with the insignia of its region or ensemble. The lapels of the happi coat usually have the logo of the en- semble. On the back is an image associated with the group, often the *mon* (decorative crest) of the family, village, or associated region. The happi coat is tied with an *obi* (sash) in a coordinated color.

Practice Clothing

During taiko practice, the most important

Festival wear.

requirement for clothing is that it be comfortable. Unlike some Japanese martial arts like karate, aikido, or kendo, it is not always required to practice taiko while wearing the traditional uniform of the dojo. Thus at a taiko dojo you are likely to see drummers in T-shirts, shorts, and other loose-fitting, but typically Western, garments.

Costumes

Most regions in Japan have a style or piece of taiko music that is considered unique to that area, village, or township. Some ensembles have taiko pieces that depict local folktales and use costumes and props to depict characters and elements of the story. This type of dramatic production is different from more formal theatrical performances, as the drummers are often enacting the storyline, rather than accompanying it. The drummers can depict *oni* (demons), ghosts, villagers, comedic figures, animals, and just about any other kind of character that might appear in the tale. One popular narrative piece performed by Gojinjo Daiko on the Noto Peninsula on the Sea of Japan tells the tale of how the villagers used cunning to stave off the onslaught of a Japanese warlord. The Lion Dance is another popular story that has become a taiko mainstay.

In some regions, the local dress is quite striking. In Okinawa, for example, Taiko groups wear the festive colors and formal hats and attire of their semitropical islands. Although women did not traditionally perform taiko except in certain areas, when they did perform they would sometimes clothe themselves in beautiful kimono. Today, women represent perhaps some 60 percent of all taiko enthusiasts worldwide, and their regalia are as diverse as their backgrounds.

A Taiko Performance

The theater lights dim. The main curtain flies open, revealing the silhouette of fifty drums and drummers kneeling in silence. On the stage, the shape of a fan is revealed—the point upstage, the drummers fanning out along the downstage edge. A lone voice sings out a note whose pitch rises, then falls. The beginning is a Shinto chant (Norito) to invoke the gods (*kami*) to come down to Earth. The Norito ends and the performers, breathing together, strike a pose in silence. A kiai (spirit voice)

cues the drummers, who all begin playing together in perfect synchronized movement on the bodies (*do*) of the drums. All stand and kiai together, the first beat falling on all fifty drum heads (*don*) as though played by only one person. The thunderous sound throws you back on your seat and reverberates through your body, as the fifty drummers play through the first of three choruses. (The number of choruses must be three, to bring good luck. Even numbers do not have the randomness of nature; four is considered especially bad luck, and it is unusual to evoke it in performance.)

Led by the bell-like cannon (tetto), the high-pitched, small, rope-tensioned drums (shime-daiko) upstage keep and accent the basic beat. Up center, the great drum (o-daiko) adds power to the downbeats. The medium-size drums (chu-daiko), about 2 feet high and wide, which cover the majority of the stage, play the melody. The second chorus speeds up and, at the end of the chorus, the vocal cue signals the team into the bridge. The o-daiko, shime-daiko, and tetto begin the bridge, and chu-daiko players begin a choreographed dance, holding the timing with kiai while playing the accent beats. As one, they build the tempo to a feverish speed, then give the kiai and together return for a final lightning round of the chorus. All drummers finish together in a final pose, their left arms outstretched high over their heads, looking toward their sticks (bachi), pointing toward the gods. As the curtain lands, the performers break their pose, connecting with the audience in traditional bows addressing first stage left, then stage right, and, finally, center.

In taiko there are four fundamental disciplines—spirit, action, body, and etiquette. (These are more fully covered in the next chapter.) Of the four, the discipline of spirit is the most important part of any taiko performance, because without it none of the others can exist. You may not literally "see" the spirit at a performance, but you will most certainly sense it in the resonance of the drum and the way the performers stand, move, and work together.

For example, many years ago, a group came from Japan to perform at the International Taiko Festival in California. They were told they had a technical rehearsal, and the whole ensemble showed up for it in full regalia, ready to present their entire performance. Worried there had been a language problem, the organizers asked if the troupe had misunderstood—the rehearsal was only for spacing, lighting, sound. The Japanese group responded that they had understood perfectly. It was merely that every time they touch the taiko, it was for the audience of their spirit, their communication with their god.

Connecting with Nature

Not all taiko is as profound as the message that was received that day, but taiko is always meant to be performed with a full spirit. And while there are elements of a taiko performance that are as organized as *ikebana* (flower arranging) and as traditional as *sado* (tea ceremony), there is also a great and spontaneous joy and celebration that comes from the playing of the drum itself.

For the audience (and the practitioner), the most important part of the live performance is to be in the moment. It is a time to share spirit and energy, to feel a part of the experience. The performers' energy inspires the audience, and the audience's energy inspires the performers. In theater, there is the concept of an invisible "fourth wall," a division between the performer and the spectator, the presence of which allows the magic of theater to occur as though there were no one watching. In taiko, the wall does not even exist.

When you are watching a taiko performance, remember that the artists are representing the human connection with nature. Learning the basic elements of nature and how they connect with taiko will go a long way toward helping you understand the various pieces you will hear.

Earth

土 The art of taiko is very much like many other Eastern martial arts. Taiko players are meant to be fully connected with the Earth and completely centered within themselves. The standing drummer strictly adheres to a *kata* (stance) that is traditional to the piece or style in which he or she plays. That stance must be held firm, so that the upper body has fluidity and the moves can be executed with precision. As an analogy, the stance represents the mountain, the body's groundedness and strength. Normally one leg is straight, the other slightly bent for balance.

A seated drummer will play in a formal *seiza* position (kneeling with the legs tucked under) but occasionally may sit cross-legged. In both cases, the posture is very stable, with the center of gravity near to the ground.

Air (Wind)

 Once the performer has built a solid foundation, the movements of the upper body need to act as a contrast. The upper body should have fluidity of motion, a sharpness of control, and the ability to rapidly change direction with force, like the wind.

Music, imagination, inspiration, and communication are the qualities associated with the element of air. The aspect of the mind is its representation. In a taiko performance, it is not only the strength that inspires, but the grace.

Fire

Each beat should be played with full spirit, whether quiet or powerful, and have the full commitment of the player. The ultimate challenge is to unite the spirit of the drummer with the spirit of the drum. Practice may consist of repeating the same beat over and over until the drummer feels the connection. The taiko player is attempting to achieve something beyond music: a sound, a movement, a spirituality that transcends the ordinary and approaches the feeling of meditation. The art,

at its finest, should allow the performer to lose himself in the here and now.

A good taiko performer will play with the fire-like qualities of passion, determination, and power.

Water

During a performance, the taiko drum itself is the container for the emotive energy that flows from the drummer like water. When the taiko is played, the performer is connecting with the spirit of the tree, the skins for the heads, and all those who created the container and each drummer to play it before.

The circle that is the shape of the drum represents nature and the divine. The circle in Asia is associated with the intuitive faculties that help humans connect with Nature (a square is associated with analytical faculties, because there are not usually visible right angles in Nature). Farmers beat the round taiko in ancient times to simulate the sound of thunder and to encourage the spirit of rain into action.

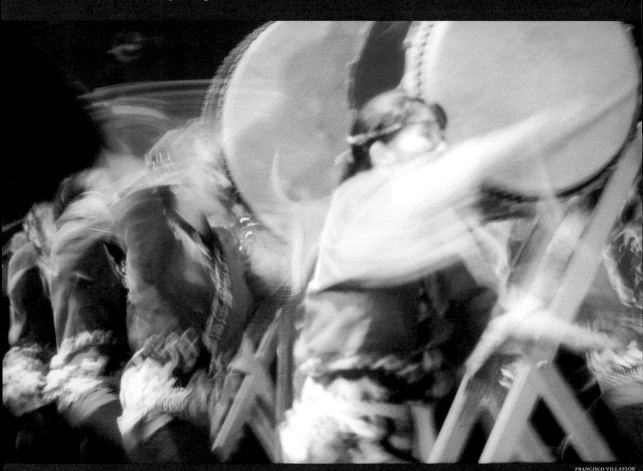

San Francisco Taiko Dojo Rising Stars.

FRANCISCO VILLAFLOR

San Francisco Taiko Dojo Rising Stars.

KALLAN NISHIMOTO

San Francisco Taiko Dojo.

FRANCISCO VILLAFLOR

FRANCISCO VILLAFLOR

San Jose Taiko.

San Francisco Taiko Dojo.

San Francisco Taiko Dojo.

FRANCISCO VILLAFLOR

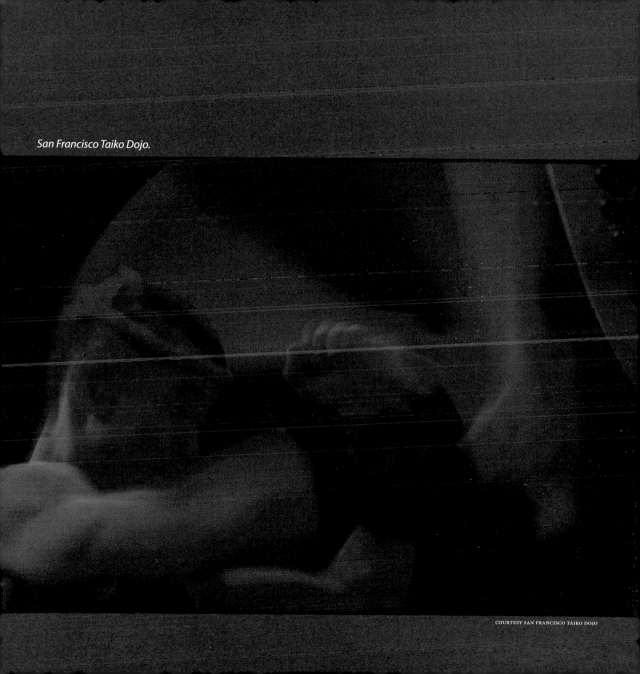

San Francisco Taiko Dojo.

San Jose Taiko.

San Francisco Taiko Dojo Rising Stars.

San Francisco Taiko Dojo.

Training in the Way

The Tale of Nafune

Some 350 years ago, Nafune on the Noto Peninsula along the Sea of Japan was a farming village blessed by the bounty of the surrounding waters. One day, the great warlord Kenshin Uesugi heard of prosperous Nafune and decided to capture it. Far in the outer fields, a lone farmer encountered the Uesugi advance scouts and heard their plan. When the village leaders were told of the imminent invasion, they were afraid. Nafune had no weapons to defend itself against the power of a great warlord. As all seemed lost, some children playing nearby the elders suggested they all disguise themselves. So artisans carved fierce masks in tree bark. The women shredded their kimono. Children gathered seaweed from the shore for everyone to wear in their hair. All the taiko in the village were brought down to the beach and bonfires were lit throughout the town. The warlord's ships at last appeared, and everyone in the village beat the taiko in a fearsome style all night long. The invading samurai, hearing the taiko and seeing the strange creatures, believed the village of Nafune to be haunted by demon drummers and sailed away, never to return. Ever since then in Nafune, every year in August, the descendants of those farmers and fishermen dress in special costumes, light bonfires and firecrackers, and play that special beat they began so many years ago. The people of the village celebrate winning a war armed only with the power of music.

Learning to Drum

The popularity of taiko in the United States has soared in the past few decades, from a handful of groups to nearly two hundred. The taiko community has had some mixed feelings about this sudden growth in interest. On the one hand, increased exposure has brought exciting new global awareness of the traditional art and the assurance that taiko will continue to develop into the future. But the accompanying excitement has also encouraged many inexperienced practitioners to begin giving instruction in the art of taiko before they are ready. Not only can this cause harm to the curious beginner, with many schools and no standardized method of instruction, but this is dangerous ground to tread upon.

The study of any traditional Japanese art is an inner journey, unique to the practitioner. Taiko is an art form you may never "master." The most important part of taiko is the journey itself.

The question to ask yourself, if you are thinking of studying taiko, is, What do I want from my experience? Personal challenge, self-confidence, meditation, aerobic workout, and discovery of a traditional art are all part of the study in any taiko group.

Many precepts of taiko are similar to those in other traditional arts. Taiko is not just about the training. One who practices must follow the Way. Practice permeates life; practice at everything you do. Spiritual development is key, and skills are merely the means to an end. To achieve your goals, you must release your mind. To practice together, you must know yourself first and then you may know others.

This book is intended merely as an introduction to the art form of taiko. Should you actually wish to begin studying, it is essential that you find a reputable instructor. Some senior groups are listed at the back of this book. The Internet, local Japanese American organizations, public and private schools, colleges, and Buddhist and other community churches are all good places to locate a taiko group. A book is a resource, a tool in guiding your questions. True study can only be accomplished by regular attendance at a dojo.

With appropriate instructors, there are no limits for practitioners. Anyone from preschoolers to senior citizens can become a student. There are exclusive performance ensembles as well as groups open to communities. If there are no taiko groups nearby your home, begin by visiting one of the many taiko-group web sites, and then you may need to be creative in your study, seeking out learning tools available online.

The following is a short course of study based on the four main elements of taiko. It is intended to further illuminate the subtleties of performance for audiences, to aid in the study for practitioners, and to encourage those who wish to try. When the taiko student trains, it is not merely to learn the rhythms or the style. The goal of the art is to reach a level inside yourself where you are truly communicating with the drum.

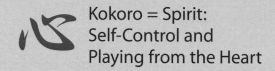

Kokoro = Spirit: Self-Control and Playing from the Heart

You must cultivate awareness of mind as well as strength of body. Attention is central to practice. Each student should seek as full a state of attentiveness as possible. The act of focusing attention can be practiced in daily life. It is a Zen concept: When you walk, just walk. When you do the dishes, only do the dishes. When you practice taiko, focus exclusively on the drum. You must be present in the moment to study taiko. Your mind must be focused. To play, you may not be scattered or confused. This is the basis of any study in the Way.

Giving your full attention to an activity leads to a frame of mind where you become so fully conscious that the sense of self may drop away. To be part of an ensemble, you must let go of all selfishness and personal focus and direct your full energy to the task at hand. Repetition of basic skills frees your mind to let go of the thoughts of playing and to focus on the experience.

When you strike the taiko, even if you are playing the precise beat with accurate skill you are not yet there. Your goal is to feel as though you are playing *through* the drum, reaching not only the side you are playing, but the opposite side. Your body must be relaxed and your breathing comfortable, even to the point where you can feel your heart with each beat.

When you play the taiko, you should feel the energy of the Earth through your feet, and a connectedness to all things. And as everything else drops away, the joy of those who built the drum, of those who played before you, will fill you. That energy will be released to the drum from the end of your bachi.

Each beat comes from your *hara* (the center of your abdomen). You must stabilize your center and focus your mental energy to a point just below your belly button. This is your center of balance and gravity, and by focusing on each beat com-

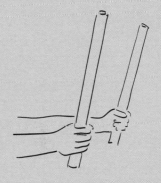

ing from this point you bring your mind and body together. There is but the one point in one moment, and you focus your full energy upon that point. Your *ki* (life spirit) is concentrated in your *hara*.

An important element of Japanese music, art, and life is *ma*, sometimes translated as "interval." In the West, the common denominator of all music is the four-beat cadence. Anthropologists relate the Western sense of beat to Occidental nomadic prehistory, a time when music was patterned by the rhythmic movement of horses and travelers.

In the East, and particularly Japan, the beat of social civilization was determined by a predominately agricultural lifestyle. Thus, the distinctly uneven rhythms of nature such as thunder, rain, wind, and earthquake became the building blocks of music. The anticipation of the thunder after seeing the lightning strike, the moments between the raindrops, the dissipation of the gale, the stillness after the tremor: this is *ma*. *Ma* is the space between the beats. It is as important as the sound, since it conveys the discipline of spirit. Anyone may beat the drum, but to have a true sense of taiko, you must learn the concept of *ma* as well.

There are two parts to a taiko performance. *Omote* is what is visible on the outside, the public face. This is a byproduct of training, not the goal. *Ura* is the invisible, what is on the inside. You must reach beyond the outside to find the subtle nuances inside. *Ura* may only be felt through experience. Until then, taiko is only the superficiality of outer skills. When you have reached the *ura*, you are moving past skill and ability to the true heart of taiko. However, *ura* does not exist without *omote*. This is the Japanese concept of visible-invisible duality, or *in-yo*. In Chinese, it is called *yin-yang*.

技 Waza = Action: Musicianship, Skill, Technique

Before you embark on your study of taiko, be mindful that improper technique will cause physical injury. You must master the *kata* (prescribed forms or stances) for each style of taiko piece before learning the music. Make sure your instructor is qualified in the style before you attempt to learn it. Just so you know, "golfers elbow" (hyperextension forward) or "tennis elbow" (hyperextension on the strike) have both earned the term "taiko elbow"!

The instructor only teaches one small aspect of the art. The application of the instruction must then be discovered by each student through incessant practice and training. Taiko is generally passed down orally, from teacher to student. The music is taught first by special words known as *kuchishoga*. For example, to strike the *hara* (center of the skin) of the nagado-daiko hard is indicated by the

Shime:	Teke	Ten	Suku	Tere	Suku	Ten	Suku	Su
Nagado:			Don		Don		Don	Don
Atarigane:	Chiki	Chi	Chan	Chan	Chiki	Chi	Chan Cha Chan	

Fue (not accurate to timing): Chi hyi hyi to ro to hyu hya

To hyu hya chi I hyi to ro

To hya to hya to i hya I to ro

To hyu hya I to i hya I to ro

Hya I to eya I to hya I to hya I to

Hya o hya o hya o chi hi hi hi

Examples of kuchishoga for the Lion Dance, showing parts for the shime- and nagado-daiko, the bells (atarigane), and flute (fue). Each syllable represents a type of sound or strike.

word "don." To strike the *fuchi* (edge of the drum) is "ka." To strike the *shime-daiko* is "ten." A silent beat is indicated by "tsu." Each note of the *fue* (flute) has a corresponding word, "chi," "hi," "hyu," etc. Similar words are used for all the instruments in a taiko ensemble.

Handle your bachi (drumsticks) every day. Familiarity breeds confidence. Your bachi should not fall. Would you drop the fingers from your hand? The proper hold is relaxed with the V of your thumb and forefinger pointing toward you. Establish the proper *kata* or stance. The drum is struck at a precise angle, the best sound being at eight o'clock and four o'clock on the head of the smaller instruments, and at ten o'clock and two o'clock when striking the wooden rim. Playing the large o-daiko when the heads are perpendicular to the floor requires the bachi to be straight, shoulder-width apart. The angle the bachi normally hits the drum should be approximately an inch off the drum head.

The various types of drumsticks, or bachi, are held in as many ways as there are stances. Normally, in kumi-daiko (ensemble drumming) they are held by the drum-

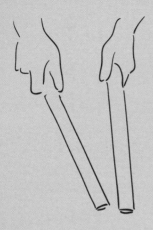

mer in the manner of traditional martial arts: from a relaxed position at the sides, the arms are raised to a *kamite* (waiting stance). The V formed by the index finger and thumb when holding the bachi points toward the drummer. The arms are extended, never folding too close to the body, which would diminish the dynamism of the strike. The stick is an extension of the body, and the line from shoulder to elbow to hand to bachi is always maintained. To deviate from the correct angle is to risk injury.

A watchful stillness is as important as activity. This is not pure silence, but what is called *zanshin*, the protracted tension after the moment of action. *Zan* means lingering, *shin* means mind. In taiko, this is the follow-through of *ki* after the completion of the technique, movement, or beat.

The concept of motion in stillness or, conversely, stillness in motion is also of great importance to the study of taiko. Timing and rhythm (*hyoshi*) are vital and are only achieved if you are relaxed. The great power of taiko and the mastery of technique can only be produced with a release of tension, especially from the upper body: shoulders, arms, wrists, hands.

Skills are improved with repetition. Personal skills are developed by practicing every day. Group skills are developed with basic exercises focusing on communication. Taiko is like hot water: if you do not constantly heat it, it will become cold.

Diversity breeds innovation; innovation fosters growth. Always follow the Way and the skill will find you.

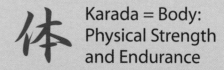

Karada = Body: Physical Strength and Endurance

Many people in the West think that taiko is an art of performance coupled with physical endurance. But, as I mentioned earlier, that is only a part of the whole. Before progressing, you must recognize that taiko is not merely what you do in the dojo. You must take the concepts learned in practice and develop them outside of the dojo.

The martial way is centered on posture. Strive to maintain balance. Breathing is an essential element. Most of us think we know how to breathe, since breathing is a natural function of life. But in our busy lives, we race along: we work, we fight deadlines, we cook, we clean, we rush. Stress makes our breathing shallow and threatens our balance.

Relearn to breathe. Several times a day, breathe in through your nose and out through your mouth. Focus on your solar plexus, the center of your body, and imagine yourself to be in balance.

In daily practice, begin by moving your body and progress to more intensive practice. Walk or run daily, practicing your breathing and building your stamina. Start slowly—10 minutes if that is all you can do—and extend your time by degrees. Never force anything unnaturally or unreasonably, but let go of your limitations. Vary your surroundings if you are able. While you are accomplishing your task, think of your breathing and try to stay in the here and now. Should your mind wander, remind yourself of your breath and your study.

Many groups practice other martial arts, calisthenics, stretching, hand and finger exercises, aerobics, or other kinds of movement. Keep up with your ensemble by building your endurance at home.

There are various postures associated with each type of drum, varying with the style of playing. You must first find your balance in your stance. Your feet should be firmly connected to the Earth. Start with your feet a bit wider than shoulder-width apart. Slightly bend your left knee, being careful not to lean over your toes; your shin should be no more than perpendicular to the ground. Rotate your left knee slightly

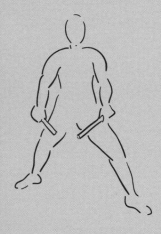

outward. Straighten your right leg, widening your stance. Tilt your hips forward and tighten your gluteus to protect your lower back. Recenter your body. The energy should flow through the Earth, to your center. Imagine that you are holding tightly to the Earth with your feet. You should not feel strain in your legs, but a comfortable tension.

Your upper body should be relaxed. Move side to side at your waist and purposefully relax your shoulders. Reach under each elbow one at a time with the opposite hand and stretch your arm across your body, relaxing your shoulder so you can feel the stretch through your neck, shoulder, and triceps. Check to see that you are maintaining your correct posture.

Now lift your unbent arms to shoulder height in front of you and imagine a drum, skin perpendicular to the floor in front of you. Your shoulder, elbow, and wrist should be in line with your imaginary drumstick. Slowly reach back with your right arm from the shoulder without bending your elbow. At the same time, twist your upper body in the same direction, so you reach the goal of having your right arm behind your right ear. Return your arm to its original shoulder-height position while twisting your upper body back toward your imaginary drum. Consciously relax your shoulders.

Repeat on the right side until you are sure you have achieved a balance in motion. Then switch to the left side and perform the same movements so that your left arm is behind your left ear. When you have at last maintained an accurate pattern, slowly alternate from right to left, breathing out on the attack, that is, on the forward motion. Build your repetitions each day, remembering your breathing, your center, and your balance—and to relax.

There are different postures used to

play the o-daiko depending on whether you are attacking forward or from the side. You can play nagado-daiko with the skin perpendicular to the floor high or low, with the skin parallel to the floor or at a 45° angle, or held between your knees while you are seated. You can play the shime-daiko standing or sitting. *Narimono* (percussion instruments) require different postures as well.

These basic postures and movements are the most important part of physical training.

礼 Rei = Etiquette: Respect, Courtesy, Unity

Dojo is a Japanese word literally meaning "the place of the Way." Taiko is traditionally learned in a dojo, although the dojo itself may in fact be just a common room in a community center. But the practice of taiko transforms the space into a place of the Way, where the long tradition of the art is transmitted from teacher to student in an atmosphere of respect and seriousness.

In a traditional dojo in Japan or elsewhere, study is carried out according to certain traditional Japanese customs of etiquette and behavior. The best way to begin your study is with a letter of introduction to a teacher or some other prearrangement through a current student.

If you are just looking around for a place to study, you will need to visit your potential dojo first and take a class. Maintain a dignified demeanor throughout practice. There is a samurai adage that states, "Behave as if the walls have eyes": you are being observed whether you realize it or not. Don't lean against your chair, fidget, look about, or talk with those around you. Avoid sitting or standing with your back to anyone. When class is complete, approach the *senpai* (senior student) or junior instructor and express gratitude for the opportunity of observation. The *senpai* will usually be seated to the right of the other students. An introduction to the *sensei* (master instructor) will then follow. Call your instructor "sensei" and demonstrate obedience, but not obsequiousness. If you are already advanced in taiko and invited to practice, sit among the juniormost students *(kohai)* of the dojo, regardless of your rank. Even if you are asked to take a more senior position, sit slightly back when placed near the students of your rank to show humility. Modesty is an important part of study, for if you believe yourself to be accomplished, you have no room to grow and your skills will plateau. Cultivate an attitude of receptivity.

I would like to expand on the concept of sensei, *senpai*, and *kohai* in Japanese culture. A sensei is an instructor whose title was bestowed by his or her instructors when the practitioner achieved a certain level of skill and was thus granted permission to teach others. The title is earned, not lightly granted, and never bestowed upon oneself. In Japan, many types of accomplished experts are referred to as "sensei":

the pharmacist, the teacher, the coach. Although the sensei is the most important person in the dojo, he is not necessarily a spiritual teacher or someone who requires that you follow his way of life. You are not trying to become like the sensei. You are trying to achieve your personal best.

Senpai and *kohai* refer to a relationship between a senior and junior. The *senpai* in a dojo are responsible for setting an example for the *kohai* to follow. They assume responsibility for instructing the *kohai* in manners and etiquette. They answer questions and help with their personal growth and with matters of dojo protocol. The *kohai* for their part are responsible for paying strict attention to the learning process. They must cultivate their powers of observation and follow the examples of the *senpai*. By their own growth, the *kohai* push their instructors forward and challenge the *senpai* to achieve. The relationship among sensei, *senpai*, and *kohai* should be one of mutual respect, demonstrated by everyday courtesy.

In a Western environment, there is sometimes more discussion, rules may be more relaxed, and practice can be very democratic. In a taiko dojo, however, the rules are more strictly observed; only in this way can there develop a mental strength and an environment conducive to personal growth. There should be no idle chatter, eating, chewing gum, smoking, or drinking in the place of study. Likewise, there is no place for jewelry, hats, sunglasses, or headphones and other electronics, which are disruptive to study and can also cause injury. Conversations should be limited to the topic of taiko.

You should bow before entering and upon leaving the dojo, which for those who train there is a sacred place. Bowing upon entry affirms your intention to train hard and seriously and upon exit to show thanks for a good session. Students should also bow to and greet instructors, assistant instructors, and guest instructors to emphasize politeness and to cultivate respect for one another. When instructors or visit-

ing instructors enter or leave, students should stop what they are doing and bow. Attentiveness is an important skill. If you have to leave for any reason during class, approach the instructor and ask permission.

All instructions from the sensei or designated instructor must be followed. Carry out directives promptly to avoid having the rest of the class wait for you. Never stand with your hands on your waist or in your pockets; the former indicates aggression, the latter laziness. Always sit cross-legged or in *seiza* (kneeling) position. Acknowledge criticism with the word *Hai!* ("Yes!"). If you are having trouble with technique, do not shout across the room to the instructor for help. Try to solve your dilemma first by careful observation. If you still have trouble, request help from a junior instructor at an appropriate moment. It is considered polite to bow upon receiving instruction or correction. Do not attempt to learn or teach new forms without the express permission of your sensei. You should report any injuries or illness to your sensei immediately.

All students are responsible for keeping the dojo tidy. For safety, the floor should always be dry, clean, and free of all objects. Each student should do his or her part to contribute to a proper training environment. Cleanliness and purity are closely connected in the Japanese arts. By ritualistic cleaning, you are not only purifying the space where you practice, but also the individuals who practice there, including yourself.

Each student is considered an integral part of the taiko community. Should it be necessary to discontinue practice for any reason, you must inform your instructors so they can have an accurate record of their students. This can be in person or in a letter, and you should always thank your instructors for their knowledge and assistance and remember that their training and support are what brought you to this point in your life. You will carry that training with you always. Herein lies the concept of *on* and *giri*. *On* refers to owing honor and gratitude to parents, seniors, ancestors, and teachers. *Giri* describes debts incurred to one's *onjin* (benefactor) and is a code of personal responsibility, loyalty, and duty. It is a crucial part of maintaining the balance between independent self-determination and responding to group needs.

You must have respect for the instruments, as well as for your taiko peers. It may seem obvious, but the taiko should never be used as a table or for playing around or in any way treated with disrespect. The skins of the drum should not be placed directly on the ground. When the taiko is stored, it should not be stored on the heads.

The above is not a list of rules, but a guide to learning. Some of the concepts are traditional Japanese techniques or manners followed for hundreds of years. Some have developed with the art form. Still others are merely common sense and common courtesy. Though there may seem to be a lot of customs to remember, they are really quite simple to maintain. Musically, however, experimentation in the proper context is encouraged—and is the only way any art form can grow.

Finally, although taiko has much in common with martial arts like karate and aikido, there are no belt levels of training. Belt levels are a product of Western goal-oriented society. You progress by degrees as you continue your learning . You are always a student of life, and always the training you receive at the dojo remains in your heart. The essence of the Way can only be realized through experience, and what you attain depends upon the purity of thought through which you attain it. The Way begins and ends with courtesy.

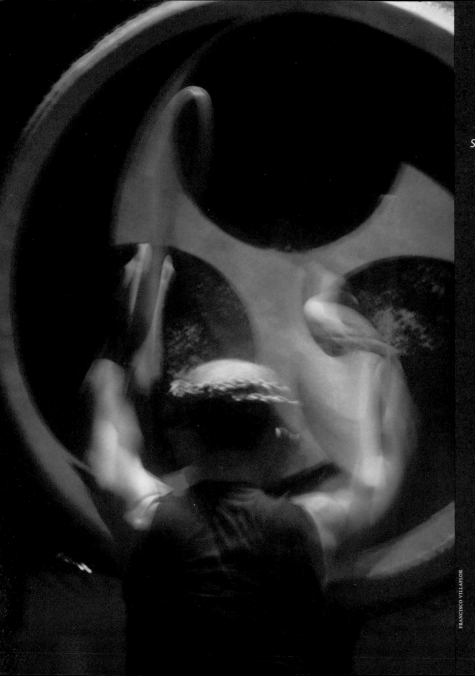

San Francisco Taiko Dojo

San Francisco Taiko Dojo.

FRANCISCO VILLAFLOR

San Francisco Taiko Dojo Rising Stars.

FRANCISCO VILLAFLOR

San Francisco Taiko Dojo.

FRANCISCO VILLAFLOR

San Jose Taiko.

San Francisco Taiko Dojo Rising Stars.

FRANCISCO VILLAFLOR

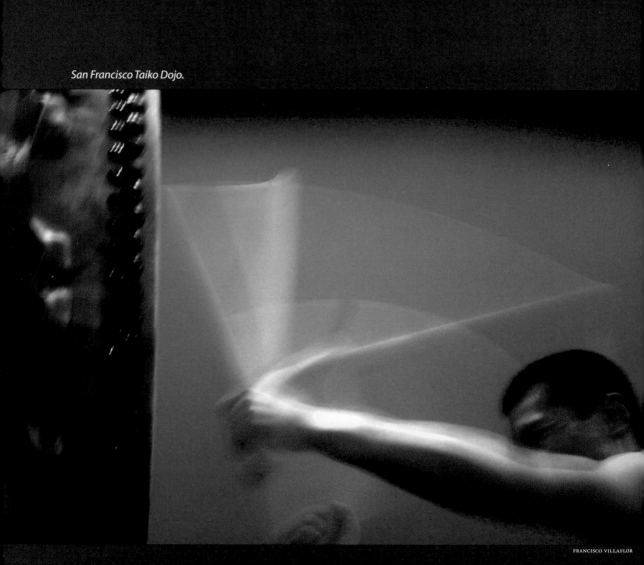

San Francisco Taiko Dojo.

FRANCISCO VILLAFLOR

San Francisco Taiko Dojo.

FRANCISCO VILLAFLOR

Kijima Daiko.

San Francisco Taiko Dojo.

FRANCISCO VILLAFLOR

San Francisco Taiko Dojo.

FRANCISCO VILLAFLOR

Seiichi Tanaka.

FRANCISCO VILLAFLOR

Ernie Reyes World Action Team.

Senior Taiko Ensembles

First Wave

Seiichi Tanaka
San Francisco Taiko Dojo (1968)
1581 Webster Street, #201
San Francisco, CA 94115

Masao Kodani and George Abe
Kinnara Taiko (1969)
Senshin Buddhist Temple
1311 West 37th Street
Los Angeles, CA 90007

PJ and Roy Hirabayashi
San Jose Taiko (1973)
P.O. Box 26895
San Jose, CA 95159

Second Wave

Aiko Kimura
Denver Taiko (1976)
c/o Tri-State Denver Buddhist Temple
1947 Lawrence Street
Denver, CO 80202

Etsuo Hongo
Los Angeles Matsuri Taiko (1977)
3821 Cherrywood Avenue
Los Angeles, CA 90008

Alan and Merle Okada, Teddy Yoshikami
Soh Daiko (1979)
332 Riverside Drive
New York, NY 10025
Jeanne Mercer and Russel Baba

Stan Shikuma
Seattle Kokon Taiko (1980)
3214 - 24th Ave S
Seattle, WA 98144

Katari Taiko (1981)
c/o Diane Kadota Arts Management
#310–425 Carrall Street
Vancouver, BC
Canada V6B 6E3

Jeanne Mercer and Russel Baba
Shasta Taiko (1985)
1723 North Old Stage Road
Mount Shasta, CA 96067

Kenny Endo
Kendo Music
758 Kapahulu Avenue, #337
Honolulu, HI 96816

A Taiko Glossary by David Leong

A

age-bachi: Wooden sticks used to tension the ropes on tsukeshime-daiko. See also *hon-jime, tate-jime*.

atarigane: Also known as *chan-chiki* or *kane*. A hand gong often used to keep time. It is played held in the hand or suspended by a cord and struck with a deer-horn mallet called the *shumoku*. It is often decorated with tassels called *fusa*.

B

bachi: Also *buchi*. General term for drumsticks. Also refers to the plectrum or pick used by shamisen and biwa players. There are a staggering variety of bachi in many sizes, shapes, and materials. The most common woods used are *kashi* for nagado-daiko, *ho* for shime-daiko, and *hinoki* for o-daiko. Almost all taiko are struck with bachi, the only exceptions being the ko-tsuzumi, o-tsuzumi, and *yoko*.

bin-sasara: Also *ita-sasara*. A ratttle-like instrument made of many small slats of wood connected by a spine of string with a handle at each end. By flicking the handles back and forth, the player causes the slats to strike each other, creating a "zipping" sound.

biwa: A round-backed lute with a cranked neck developed from the Chinese *pipa* and played with an oversized plectrum. The biwa has three strings and four frets. Often played in conjunction with the singing of old historical tales, e.g., *Heike Monogatari*, but also a solo instrument in its own right.

bo-sasara. A long, notched stick that is rubbed with a smaller stick.

bu: Traditional Japanese measure. 10 *bu* make 1 *sun*. Subdivided into 10 units called *rin*. Roughly equivalent to 0.118 inches in the Kana system. See also *shaku*.

bubinga: English name for the *toboku* tree of West Camaroon.

Bugaku: Classical Japanese court dance. Accompanied by Gagaku music. The dances are divided into Dances of the Left and Dances of the Right. *See also* Gagaku, Sahogaku, Uhogaku.

buna: The Japanese beech tree. Used for bachi.

busho-dai: A low, lightweight stand used to hold a classical shime-daiko at a slight angle. Used while playing the shime-daiko from a seated position. Similar to, but slightly heavier and sturdier than, a *teren-dai*.

buyo: Classical Japanese dance.

byo: Tacks used to nail the heads on certain taiko.

byo-daiko: Also *byo-uchi-daiko*. General term for a nailed-head drum.

C

cannon: *See* tetsu-zutsu.

chan-chiki: *See* atarigane.

chappa: Also called *tebyoshi*. Small hand cymbals. Size given in units of *go* where 1 *go* is equal to 1 *sun*. Usual sizes range from 4 *go* to 6 *go*.

chochin: Paper lantern. Used for decoration by some taiko groups. It is common to have the taiko group's name written on the *chochin*.

chogake: A system of measurement for tsukeshime-daiko. There are 4 *chogake* sizes, from 2 *chogake* to 5 *chogake*: 2-*chogake* drums have lighter bodies and thinner heads; 5-*chogake* drums have the heaviest bodies and thickest heads and are capable of a much higher pitch. Sometimes the term is colloquially shortened to *cho*. In addi-tion to the *chogake* sizes, there is the lightest tsukeshime called *namitsuke*. See also *namitsuke,* tsukeshime-daiko.

chu-daiko: General term for a medium-size drum, roughly 2 *shaku* in diameter. It most often refers to a drum of that size in the nagado-daiko style.

D

da-daiko: Highly decorated oke-daiko style drum used for Gagaku and religious ceremonies. The drum is placed in an ornately carved frame and is played with short, padded beaters. *Da-daiko* are usually around 6 feet in diameter and are one of the oldest styles of taiko used in Japan, dating from at least the 7th century. There are two styles of *da-daiko*, and they are always played in pairs. The Leftside (*saho*) *da-daiko* and the Rightside (*uho*) *da-daiko*. The *saho da-daiko* has a green body and a *futatsu-domoe* is lacquered on the head, and the stand has images of a phoenix surmounted by a carved sun. The *uho da-daiko* has a red body and a *mitsu-domoe* lacquered on the head, and the stand has Chinese dragons surmounted by a carved moon.

dai: General term for a drum stand. Also used as a suffix in a compound word indicating the style of stand: e.g., *shikaku-dai* is a stand of *shikaku* (square) shape.

daibyoshi: A style of short-bodied oke-daiko used in Kabuki music. Usually lacquered black. The high pitch of the drum is used to represent the atmosphere and ambience of Edo and city life. See also *tsuchibyoshi*.

-daiko: Suffix used to indicate a type of drum, a taiko group, or a style of taiko playing in a compound word. Examples: chu-daiko (medium-size taiko); Osuwa Daiko (the Osuwa taiko group); Miyake-daiko (the style of taiko playing in the Miyake region).

do: Sometimes spelled "doh" (English variant). General term used for the body of a drum.

do: "The Way." Indicates a path of learning.

dojo: A place for studying. Lit.: "the place of the Way." A taiko dojo would be a place for learning taiko.

dora: A fairly small gong with a deep lip and pronounced center boss.

E

Edo-bayashi: Festival music of Edo (old Tokyo).

eisa-daiko: Okinawan style of Bon dancing and drumming. Known for its spirited drumming, often by dancers who carry the drums as they dance.

F

fuchi: The rim of the drum, where the "ka" note is played.

fue: In the broadest meaning, any blown instrument including nokan, shakuhachi, and sho. However, the term is widely used to refer to a transverse (horizontal) bamboo flute. These fue come in a variety of sizes, numbered from #1 (lowest in pitch) to #13 (highest in pitch). Most fue have six or seven holes. Most are in a native scale (*matsuribue*) but some are made to play Western scales (*utabue*). See also *matsuribue, shinobue, takebue, utabue, yokobue*.

fundoshi: A loincloth. Sometimes worn in various festivals and by some taiko groups during performances, particularly o-daiko solos.

fusa: A tassel, used as a decorative element. Often hung from the ends of atarigane cords and from chappa.

fuse-dai: A stand for a large hira-daiko. The hira-daiko is laid horizontally on a T-shaped base and supported at a slight angle by short uprights at each end of the T. Usually on casters for easy movement.

futatsu-domoe: A design made up of two comma-shaped marks in a circle (similar to a *yin-yang* symbol). Also commonly called a *tomoe.* Associated with the Music of the Left in Gagaku, it is a common design lacquered on the heads of o-daiko. See also *mitsu-domoe, tomoe.*

G

Gagaku: Japanese imperial court orchestral music. Lit.: "refined music." Introduced into Japan in the 6th and 7th centuries, and formalized in 701. The music and dances of Gagaku were organized into the Music of the Left and the Music of the Right in the 9th century. The genre exists mostly unchanged to this day, making it the oldest surviving tradition of court music still played. Gaguku utilizes a scale of seven tones and has six keys. *See also* Bugaku, *dadaiko, gaku-daiko, ikko, kakko,* Sahogaku, *sanko, shoko,* Uhogaku.

gaku-daiko: A type of highly decorated hira-daiko used in Gagaku. It is suspended vertically in a frame and struck with padded mallets. It is played while seated.

H

hachimaki: Headband often worn during festivals or by some taiko groups.

hanten: Short kimono-like coat often used in festivals and performances.

happi: Short kimono-like coat often used in festivals and performances.

hara: Belly. Location of the *ki* energy in humans. Also refers to the center of the drumhead.

harakake: Also *maekake.* An apron-like garment used in festivals and by some taiko groups.

hara-maki: Long strip of cotton cloth used to wrap the stomach or midsection.

harisen: Also *hariogi.* A short, narrow, leather-wrapped paddle used as bachi. Used in traditional instruction to learn rhythms and practice.

hayashi: General term for a musical ensemble that includes drums; musical accompaniment; festival music.

hayashi-bue: Bamboo transverse flute used in *hayashi* music. Also know as fue, *matsuri-bue, shinobue, takebue,* or *yokobue. See also* fue.

hayashi-daiko: See *o-hayashi-daiko.*

himo: Rope or cord.

hinoki: Japanese cypress tree. The wood is used for making bachi.

hira-dai: A stand for a nagado-daiko. It consists of two pieces of crossed wood that hold the drum vertically and slightly off the floor.

hira-daiko: General term for a drum that is wider than it is deep (lit.: "flat drum"), with nailed heads and carved from a single block of wood. Small hira-daiko are often used in *hayashi* music. Highly decorated versions called *gaku-daiko* are used in Gagaku. Hira-daiko have also been scaled up to o-daiko size for use by kumi-daiko groups.

hira-tsuri-daiko: A hira-daiko suspended vertically in a frame-like stand. Classified separately from the *gaku-daiko*.

ho: A soft and light wood related to the magnolia tree. Used to make bachi.

Hogaku: Japanese classical music. Associated with Nagauta and theater music. Primary instruments are the shamisen, ko-tsuzumi, o-tsuzumi, shime-daiko, and nokan.

hon-bari: The final stretching of the head over a taiko body in preparation of tacking it in place. See also *kari-bari*.

hon-jime: The final stage of tensioning a tsukeshime-daiko. Two people take turns pulling the slack out of the tensioning rope while pounding on the rope with a stick called an *agebachi*. See also *tate-jime*.

horagai: A large shell used as trumpet-type instrument. The horagai is not a conch shell, but either a Pacific triton or a shank shell.

hozonkai: A preservation society: a Japanese organization dedicated to preserving and handing down a particular tradition. Some *hozonkai* are recognized and organized as Intangible Cultural Properties; others are loosely organized guilds adhering to some formal structure, often within the context of a festival's (Shinto/Buddhist/other) historical roots or related art forms (*minyo* or folk song traditions, for example).

hyoshigi: Wooden blocks used as clappers. Similar to latin clave sticks, but struck at the tips rather than in the middle of the block.

I

ikko: A highly decorated hourglass-shaped drum used in Bugaku. Two heads are stitched onto steel rings and then laced to the body with a cord (*o-shirabe*). A tensioning cord (*ko-shirabe*) is then wound around the *o-shirabe*. The *ikko* is slung across the chest of Bugaku dancers and played with bachi in both hands. It is similar to, but smaller than, the *sanko*. See also *kakko*, *sanko*.

ippon ashi-dai: Lit.: "one legged stand." An ornate stand for a nagado-daiko used in temples and shrines.

ita-sasara: See *bin-sasara*.

J

jikata: Someone who plays the *ji* rhythm. See also *ouchi*.

jiuchi: Also called *ji*. A base or backing rhythm. Usually a simple duple beat (do ko), a swing beat (don go), or a horse rhythm (don doko).

jo: Traditional Japanese unit of measure. 10 *shaku* make 1 *jo*. About 12 feet in the Kana system. See also *kanajaku, shaku*.

josuke: Also *jozuke*. A specialized term created by Oedo Sukeroku Daiko and used to describe a medium-size (about 1.6 *shaku*) nagado-daiko on a slant stand. The term literally means to "place facing up."

K

kaba: Birchwood. Used for bachi, particularly children's bachi since it is lightweight and strong.

Kabuki: A style of theater popularized in the 1600s. Kabuki is marked by an exaggerated style compared to Noh theater, which preceded and influenced it. While originated by a woman, women were quickly banished from the stage and now all roles are performed by men.

Kabuki-bayashi: The music of Kabuki theater. The ensemble itself is called *debayashi*. Kabuki instrumentation is divided into onstage and *geza* (offstage) players. The onstage musicians are in full view of the patrons and provide the musical accompaniment. The onstage instrumentation includes fue, shamisen, *wa-daiko* (shime-daiko), ko-tsuzumi, and o-tsuzumi. The offstage musicians are backstage and provide sound effects and mood. See also *daibyoshi*, o-daiko, *tsuchibyoshi*.

kagura suzu: A decorative, hand-held bell tree comprising three tiers of jingle bells. The first (top) tier has three bells, the second tier has five, and the third tier has seven. The emphasis on odd numbers is a Buddhist influence and shows the *kagura suzu*'s religious origin.

kakegoe: Vocal calls. Used to accent the music, to signal shifts in rhythm, and to encourage other performers. *See also* kiai.

kakko: A small, highly ornate taiko used in Gagaku. Two heads are stitched onto steel rings and are then laced to a slightly rounded cylindrical body with a cord (*o-shirabe*). Two tensioning cords (*ko-shirabe*) are then wound around the *o-shirabe*. The *kakko* is set on a low stand and played by the ensemble leader who in each hand holds a thin, hardwood bachi with a slightly bulbous tip. The main function of the *kakko* is to keep time. It is associated with the Music of the Left. See also *ikko*, *sanko*.

kamae: A stance.

kan: Also *kanagu*. The ring-shaped handles attached to nailed-head taiko. Composed of two parts: *zagane* is the decorative metal plate; *kanamaru* is the ring itself.

kanajaku: "Kana *shaku*," one form of the traditional *shaku/sun* measuring system. 1 *shaku* in the Kana system is about 1 foot. The system is used to measure taiko as well as in carpentry. See also *shaku*.

kane: A gong or large bell. Also used colloquially to refer to the atarigane.

kari-bari: A prestretch of a head over the body of a taiko. See also *hon-bari*.

kashi: The Japanese oak tree. The hard and dense wood of the white oak tree (*shirogashi*) is used for bachi and *dai*.

kashu: General term for a singer.

kata: Form or style. In taiko, *kata* refers to the stances and movements used for a particular song or style. For example, the *kata* for Miyake-daiko is very different from that of Midare-uchi.

kawa: Leather, skin (for drumheads).

keyaki: The zelkova tree, which is native to Japan and grows widely throughout the islands of Honshu, Shikoku, and Kyushu. A relative of the elm, it is used extensively for *kuri-nuki-daiko* in Japan due to its hard wood and beautiful grain pattern. The best trees for taiko making are reputed to come from the foot of Mt. Haku and from the Japan Alps.

ki: Your body's energy or spirit.

kiai: A shout used to channel *ki*. Often used as kakegoe.

ko-daiko: A general term referring to a small taiko in the 1-*shaku* range.

koshi: Hips.

koto: Japanese zither, usually with thirteen strings, although bass and custom versions with more strings are also found.

ko-tsuzumi: A small hand drum. Two heads are sewn over steel rings and laced onto an hourglass-shaped body with a cord called the *shirabeo*. A second cord wraps around the first, allowing the ko-tsuzumi to be tuned. The body is made from cherry wood and is often beautifully decorated with *makie* (gilded patterns on lacquer). The pitch can be varied by squeezing the ropes with the left hand while striking the drum with the right. The drum is held in the left hand and placed on the right shoulder, and the right hand sweeps up to the shoulder to hit the head. The heads are very thin (being made from the skin of an unborn calf where possible) and are decorated with black lacquer. The best ones are reputed to have been broken in for over 100 years. Used traditionally in Kabuki, Nagauta, and Noh theater, but very rarely in kumi-daiko.

kuchishoga: Also *kuchishoka, kuchishowa*. The mnemonic syllables (and system) used in learning traditional Japanese music. One syllable will correspond to one sound/note of an instrument.

kumi-daiko: Lit.: "grouped drums." A taiko ensemble. The modern style of taiko playing using many drums and performers at the same time. The origin of this style is attributed to Daihachi Oguchi of Osuwa Daiko.

kuri-nuki-daiko: General term for a drum that has been carved out of a single log.

kusu: Camphor wood.

M

ma: The space between two events (two notes or beats on the drum, etc.). Somewhat equivalent to a rest in Western notation, but with a deeper connotation than the mere absence of sound. *Ma* is just as important as the notes that surround it, giving shape and contrast to the sounds that we hear. A very important concept in many traditional Japanese arts, not just music.

matsuri: Festival.

matsuribue: Festival flute. A fue that is used in a *matsuri* (festival) and is tuned to the requirements of that festival's music.

meari: A generic term used to indicate any wood for making taiko that is not *keyaki*. Usually applied to nagado and hira-daiko. *Meari* taiko are not as expensive as taiko made from *keyaki*. *Meari* can include horse chestnut, *toboku, sen*, and camphor among others. Lit.: "has grain." See also *keyaki*.

men: Japanese traditional mask, usually made of wood or paper. There are many kinds of *men* including those that portray demons, animals, or people. Some examples of traditional taiko styles that use masks include Gojinjo-daiko, Namahage-daiko, Shi shi Odori, and Gonbei-daiko.

mimi: The portion of the drum head below the tacks, where rods have been passed through slits in the skin. After the head has been tacked on, the *mimi* can be trimmed off or left on. If the *mimi* is removed, the option to retension the head at a later date is lost.

minyo: General term for folk music.

mitsu-domoe: A design similar to the *futatsu-domoe*, but using three comma-shaped marks contained in a circle rather than two. This design is associated with the Music of the Right in Gagaku. It is a common design lacquered on the heads of o-daiko. See also *futatsu-domoe, tomoe*.

miya-dai: A stand for a miya-daiko. The *miya-dai* has two main vertical supports and decoratively carved "wings" that cradle the taiko. The *miya-dai* holds the taiko horizontally at about waist level.

miya-daiko: Shrine or temple drum. Also used as a general term for nagado-daiko.

miyake-dai: Also *za-dai*. A low stand used to hold a nagado-daiko horizontally at knee height. Used for the Miyake style of taiko playing.

Miyake-daiko: A traditional style of taiko playing that involves low, lunging stages.

mojiri: Bachi used to twist the tensioning ropes of a taiko when its head is being put on.

momohiki: Pants often worn during festivals or by some taiko groups.

N

naga-bachi: Long bachi. Often made of tapered oak or from bamboo slats.

nagado-daiko: Lit.: "long-bodied taiko." This is the prototypical taiko drum most often associated with taiko drumming. While the term can be applied to many taiko, including some okedo, most people associate the term nagado-daiko with a taiko carved from a single piece of wood, usually *keyaki, sen, shiogi,* or *tamo.* The body has a rounded, barrel-shaped appearance, with the maximum diameter being roughly equal to the length of the drum from head to head. The cowhide heads are nailed onto the body of the drum with tacks. The pitch of the drum cannot be changed without retensioning and retacking the head in place. A pair of ring-shaped handles, called *kan,* are attached to the sides. Nagado-daiko are available in many sizes, from 1 foot to over 6 feet. A wide variety of stands are also available for this taiko.

Nagauta: A form of Japanese classical music, focusing on long songs and with shamisen and vocal melodic lines supported by percussion. The percussion ensemble includes ko-tsuzumi, o-tsuzumi, and shime-daiko. *See also* Kabuki-bayashi.

namitsuke: The lightest and smallest tsukeshime-daiko. Not capable of high pitches like the heavier *chogake*-size tsukeshime-daiko. See also *chogake,* tsukeshime-daiko, *wa-daiko.*

narimono: General term for small, handheld percussion instruments.

nawa: Rope.

nenbutsu-daiko: A style of okedo-daiko used in Kabuki and folk music. The heads are stretched directly onto the body of the taiko with rope instead of first being stitched onto steel rings and then laced to the body.

nihon ashi-dai: A low stand used to hold a shime-daiko at a slight angle. Used while playing the shime-daiko from a seated position.

nogaku: The music associated with Noh. The instrumentation includes taiko (shime-daiko), ko-tsuzumi, o-tsuzumi, and nokan.

Noh: A style of theater developed in the 1400s and influenced by Zen. Known for its use of masks and stately pace.

nokan: A flute used in Noh performances, known for its sharp sound and three-octave range. Made from many fine pieces of split bamboo in a complicated and involved process, nokan have a distinct, lacquered appearance.

O

obi: Sash or belt used to hold a kimono or *hanten* closed.

o-daiko: Lit.: "big fat drum." In general, the term is used for any drum larger than 33 inches in diameter. It can refer to a large drum of any style but usually is reserved for drums of the nagado style. In Kabuki the o-daiko is usually a nagado-daiko and is played offstage; certain rhythmic patterns are played on it for sound effects and to create a mood. Okinawan Eisa-daiko also refers to its largest drum as o-daiko although it is only about 1.5 *shaku* (about 1.5 feet) in size. This Okinawan o-daiko is shaped roughly like a nagado-daiko, but uses a stave construction from pine; this light weight allows the drum to be slung from the shoulder and played while dancing.

odori: A dance. Also a general term for Japanese dance.

o-hayashi-daiko. See *sairei-nagado*.

ojime: A type of okedo-daiko, but with a thicker head and longer body. *Ojime* is the typical okedo used by many performing taiko groups.

o-kawa: *See* o-tsuzumi.

oke: A Japanese-style barrel, made with thin slats of Japanese cypress or cedar, usually in a straight-sided, cylindrical style. It is different from *oke*-style wooden tubs.

okedo-daiko: Also oke-daiko. General term for drums made from a barrel-stave construction (not to be confused with the North American wine barrel taiko). The heads are usually stitched over steel rings and then laced to the body with a rope, similar to the shime-daiko. The tone of the drum can be changed by the rope tension. There are several styles of okedo daiko, many with a relatively long body. *Nebuta, nanbu-yo,* and *ojime* are long-body styles; the leather of the heads gets thicker, and the bodies get longer as you go from *nebuta* to *ojime*. The drums are often played horizontally on tall stands, with a player striking each head. *Daibyoshi, tsuchibyoshi,* and *nenbutsu* okedo are much shorter and are played in Kabuki and folk music. They are often held horizontally by a player seated on the floor. Eitetsu-gata (Eitetsu-style) drums are relatively short and are played vertically like the floor tom of a drum kit.

omikoshi: A portable Shinto shrine carried about on the shoulders of festival participants.

oritatami-dai: Also called *naname-dai, sukeroku-dai,* slant stand. A stand for a nagado-daiko that holds the taiko at a roughly forty-five-degree angle at waist level. Widely used by kumi-daiko groups and popularized by Oedo Sukeroku Taiko.

oroshi: A drum pattern of increasingly rapid beats, often leading to a drum roll.

o-tsuzumi: Also *o-kawa*. A small hand drum used in Noh, Nagauta, and Kabuki theater. Two heads are stitched over steel rings, placed on an hourglass-shaped body, and then laced together with rope. The body is made from cherry wood and is often beautifully decorated with *makie* (gilded patterns on lacquer). Similar to, but slightly larger than, the ko-tsuzumi, it produces a higher pitch but one that cannot be changed. The heads are made with much thicker leather than the ko-tsuzumi's and are undecorated. The drum is sometimes played with a hard papier-mâché cap called *saku* placed over the fingers, or with a short leather paddle.

ouchi: Someone who plays the main rhythm. See also *jikata*.

P

paranku: Small one-headed drum somewhat similar to a robust tambourine with no jingles. Played in Okinawan Eisa-style drumming.

R

rin: Traditional Japanese measure: 10 *rin* make 1 *bu*. Roughly equivalent to 0.1 inch in the Kana system. See also *shaku*.

ryomenbari etsuki-daiko: A small hira-daiko on a wooden handle. Held in one hand while played with a bachi in the other, it is usually around 7.5–9.5 inches in diameter. A variant called *ameya-daiko* (lit.: "candy seller's taiko") also exists, larger in diameter and thinner.

ryuteki: Flute similar in appearance and construction to the nokan, used in Gagaku.

S

Sahogaku: Music of the Left. The body of Gagaku music and dances were organized into the Music of the Right and the Music of the Left in the 9th century. Sahogaku includes Gagaku compositions from China and Southeast Asia, as well as Japanese compositions in those styles. Visually, Sahogaku is associated with the color red, the *mitsu-domoe*, and the images of dragons surmounted by the sun. See also *da-daiko*, Gagaku, Samai, Uhogaku, Umai.

sairei-nagado: Also *ohayashi-daiko*. A style of nagado-daiko that has a longer body than normal (more "cigar shaped" than round). Used for festivals, it is available in a limited range of sizes.

saku: Hard papier-mâché caps worn on the fingers and used to strike the o-tsuzumi.

Samai: Dances of the Left. Samai includes dances from China and Southeast Asia as well as Japanese compositions in that style and is always accompanied by Sahogaku. Samai generally have slow, elegant movements, which are based on the melody. Visually, Samai is associated with the color red. *See also* Gagaku, Sahogaku, Uhogaku, Umai.

sanbon ashi-dai: Lit.: "three leg dai." A low stand that holds a hira-daiko at a slight angle. Used to play the hira-daiko while seated.

sanko: Also called *san no tsuzumi*. A highly decorated hourglass-shaped drum used in Gagaku. Two heads are stitched onto rings, which are then laced to the body with a cord (*o-shirabe*). A tensioning cord (*ko-shirabe*) is then wound around the *o-shirabe*. It is played on a low stand using a slender hard-wood bachi held in the right hand, although it was once played by dancers similar to the *ikko*. Associated with the Music of the Right, it is used instead of the *kakko* in the orchestra when Bugaku dances of the Right are played. It is similar to, but larger than, the *ikko*. See also *ikko*, *kakko*.

sanshin: A banjo-like instrument with three strings. Similar to the shamisen, which it inspired. The *sanshin* is smaller, is played with a pick rather than a plectrum, and is skinned with rock snake rather than cat or dog. It originated in Okinawa, inspired by an instrument from Thailand. *See also* shamisen.

sen: Japanese wood used in making taiko. Softer, less durable, and less expensive than *keyaki*. Used in making *kuri-nuki* taiko.

shaku: Traditional Japanese measure. Each shaku is subdivided into 10 units called *sun*;

10 *shaku* make 1 *jo*. There are several different *shaku*-measuring systems depending on the industry or region of Japan. Taiko are measured using the Kana *shaku* system where 1 *shaku* is equivalent to roughly 1 foot. Kana is also the system used for carpentry. "Kujira" *shaku* in the Kujira system—not used to measure taiko—are longer, about 15 inches.

shakuhachi: Bamboo end-blown flute, with four holes in front and one in back. It takes its name from the standard instrument size of 1 *shaku*, 8 (*hachi*) *sun*, although there is a wide variety of sizes. Known for its delicate tonal shadings and evocative, breathy sounds.

shamisen: A banjo-like instrument with three strings, played with a plectrum or a pick. Often claimed to be the best instrument to express Japanese sensitivities and feelings, it is common on the Japanese main islands and developed from the Okinawan *sanshin*. The shamisen is larger and heavier than the *sanshin* and is skinned with cat or dog. See also *sanshin*.

shime-daiko: General term for a rope-tensioned drum (now sometimes bolt- or turnbuckle-tensioned as well). Also specifically refers to small rope-tuned drums often used in Noh, Kabuki, *hayashi*, kumi-daiko, etc. A shime-daiko has two heads that are sewn over steel rings and laced to a *kurinuki* body with a rope called the *shirabeo*. It is tensioned with a second rope called the *ueshirabe* that is wound around the lacings of the first rope. These shime-daiko are sometime just called "taiko" or *wa-daiko*, and have relatively thin heads, often with a circular patch of deer skin in the middle. Shime-daiko used for folk music and kumi-daiko are called tsukeshime-daiko; they are usually much heavier, have thicker skin, and are capable of being tensioned to a very high pitch. *See also* tsukeshime-daiko.

shinobue: Also known as fue, *hayashi-bue*, *takebue*, or *yokobue*. Bamboo transverse flute. *See also* fue.

shi shi daiko: A type of short okedo-daiko used in *shi shi odori*. Usually lacquered black.

shi shi gashira: Carved wooden mask of a stylized lion's head used in *shi shi mai*. Often used in male/female pairs, with the female mask typically being 1 *sun* (1.18 inches) larger than the male. The male is called *uzu*, and the female is called *gonkuro*. *Uzu* can be recognized by a prominent ridge on the top of his head. The masks are usually lacquered in vermillion or gold.

shi shi mai: Traditional lion dance. This dance,

the roots of which are in China, has an incredible amount of regional variations. The dancer, usually accompanied by taiko and fue, is hidden by a cape (*tanmono*) attached to the *shishi gashira*, which is held in the dancer's hands.

shi shi odori: Traditional deer dance. There are many regional variations of this dance. The dancer usually plays a drum hung from the waist while dancing and wears some sort of deer mask; he sometimes supports long bamboo rods that are strapped to the back and slapped on the ground with a quick bend of the waist.

sho: A mouth organ with many pipes and reeds based on the Chinese *sheng*. The reeds are similar to a harmonica's in that they can be sounded by inhaling and exhaling. Used in Gagaku.

shoko: A type of *kane* used in Gagaku. Similar in shape to atarigane but larger and suspended vertically in an ornate stand. Played with two thin sticks with bead-shaped tips.

shumoku: Also *shimoku*. Deer-horn mallet used to play the atarigane.

sugi: Japanese cedar wood. Used for oke-daiko bodies.

sumo-daiko: Small nagado-style taiko used for performing before and after sumo wrestling matches. They are played with long bamboo sticks and have a characteristic high, taut sound. While lacquered and gold-leafed versions are used for sumo, unadorned versions have found their way into kumi-daiko.

sun: Traditional Japanese measure. 10 *sun* make 1 *shaku*. Subdivided into 10 units called *bu*. Equivalent to 1.18 inches in the Kana system. See also *shaku*.

suwari-dai: Literally, "seated stand." A low stand used to hold a shime-daiko at a slight angle and used while playing from a seated position. It typically refers to a stand made from bent iron rods used to hold heavier tsukeshime-daiko.

suzu: A bell similar to a jingle bell. See also *kagura suzu*.

T

tabi: Split-toed socks worn with Japanese dress, such as kimono. *Tabi* with rubber soles are known as *jika-tabi*. *Tabi* are usually either white, black, or a very dark navy blue. They are measured not only in centimeters for length, but also in the number of *hazuse* (clasps/hook and eye closures) that close the *tabi* around the ankle. *Tabi* with four, five, and seven clasps are common. They are the favored footware for many taiko groups.

tachi-dai: An upright stand used to hold a shime-daiko at a slight angle at waist level.

taiko: General term for Japanese drums. Specifically refers to the shime-daiko used in classical Japanese music. Also used to refer to the kumi-daiko style of taiko drumming.

take: Bamboo.

takebue: Bamboo transverse flute. Also known as fue, *hayashi-bue, shinobue,* and *yokobue. See also* fue.

tamo: A wood used in taiko making.

taru: A wooden tub or barrel. Made from thick staves, usually with a tapered body, it is used for making pickles or miso paste. It is sometimes played with wooden mallets by certain Japanese traditional groups instead of taiko. The term also refers to the wine barrels used by many North American groups to make taiko, e.g., "wine-daru-daiko."

tate-jime: First step in the process of tensioning a tsukeshime-daiko. The rope passing from head to head is tightened by prying with a stick and taking up the slack. See also *hon-jime.*

tebyoshi: See chappa.

tekko: Wristbands. Often extending to cover the back of the hands.

tenugui: A cotton handcloth, often rolled up and used as a headband.

teren-dai: A low, lightweight stand that holds a classical shime-daiko at a slight angle. It is used while playing the shime-daiko from a seated position in Noh, Kabuki, Nagauta, etc.

tetsu-zutsu: Also *tetto.* Three different diameters of metal pipe (usually around 6, 8, and 10 inches) welded together to make a bell-like instrument. It is placed on a waist-high stand and played with bachi or slim metal rods. Used to keep time and signal rhythm changes, it originated with Osuwa Daiko.

toboku: Hardwood from Cameroon used as a replacement for *keyaki* wood. Used primarily for o-daiko due to the great diameters of bole available.

tochi: The Japanese horse chestnut tree. Softer, less durable, and less expensive than *keyaki.* Used for *kuri-nuki* taiko.

tomoe: A comma-shaped design, common in Japanese, Korean, and Chinese history. The term *tomoe* is commonly used when referring to a design with two of the comma-shaped marks contained in a circle (similar to a *yin-yang* symbol), although this is properly called a *futatsu-domoe* (lit.: two *tomoe*). The *tomoe* is a common design lacquered on the heads of o-daiko. See also *futatsu-domoe, mitsu-domoe.*

torii-dai: A frame-like stand that holds a hira-daiko in a vertical position.

tsuchibyoshi: A style of okedo-daiko used in Kabuki music. The low pitch of the drum is used to represent the atmosphere and ambience of the countryside. This taiko is also used in folk Shinto shrine music. See also *daibyoshi*.

tsukeshime-daiko: A type of shime-daiko used in folk or kumi-daiko playing. It is heavier and stronger and can be pitched much higher than other styles of shime-daiko. There are five sizes: *namitsuke* (thinnest heads, smallest body) and 2, 3, 4, and 5 *chogake* (thickest heads, biggest body). Tsukeshime-daiko are tensioned with a single rope system, bolts, or turnbuckles.

tsuri-dai: A stand for hira-daiko. The hira-daiko is suspended vertically in a frame, usually knee or waist high.

tsuri-daiko: A type of hira-daiko used in Gagaku. It is struck with padded mallets and is usually highly decorated. Also called a *gaku-daiko*.

tsuzumi: General term for hourglass-shaped drums.

U

uchite: A taiko player.

uchiwa-daiko: A handheld taiko that has the skin stretched and stitched over a hoop and attached to a handle. This taiko has no resonator. Lit.: "fan drum." It was originally used to accompany chanting in the Nichiren Buddhist sect but is now common in taiko groups. Most uchiwa are small (8 inches), but large versions (up to 5 feet or more) are sometimes made. Commonly set up in a rack and played as a set.

Uhogaku: Music of the Right. The body of Gagaku music and dances were organized into the Music of the Right and the Music of the Left in the 9th century. Uhogaku includes Gagaku compositions from Korea, as well as Japanese compositions in that style. Visually, Uhogaku is associated with the color green, the *futatsu-domoe*, and the image of a phoenix surmounted by the moon. See also *da-daiko*, Gagaku, Sahogaku, Samai, Umai.

Umai: Dances of the Right. Umai includes dances from Korea as well as Japanese compositions in that style, always accompanied by Uhogaku. Umai generally have more spirited movements, which are based on the rhythm. Umai also includes some humorous pieces. Visually, Umai is associated with the color green. *See also* Gagaku, Sahogaku, Samai, Uhogaku.

urushi: Japanese lacquer. The most common finish for taiko bodies, it comes in a variety of tints, from clear to black. The application of *urushi* is considered an art form in Japan. The lacquer is tapped from trees similar to the way maple syrup is obtained. The wet lacquer is also a strong irritant, being a relative of poison oak, and produces serious rashes if accidentally touched to bare skin (it is safe when dry).

uta: A song. Also a general term for singing.

utabue: A fue tuned to Western scales.

W

wa-daiko: Lit.:, "Japanese drum." The term refers in general to Japanese drums as opposed to Western percussion. Specifically it refers to the shime-daiko used in Noh and Kabuki theater. It is sometimes used to refer to kumi-daiko.

waraji: Sandals made from rice straw.

X

X-dai: An X-shaped stand for nagado and oke-daiko. The X-dai holds the taiko horizontally at head level.

Y

yagura-dai: A stand for a nagado-daiko that has four slightly splayed legs. The *yagura-dai* holds the drum horizontally at about shoulder height.

yokobue: A transverse bamboo flute. Also known as fue, *hayashi-bue, shinobue,* and *takebue. See also* fue.

yonbyoshi: The four instruments of Nogaku: ko-tsuzumi, o-tsuzumi, taiko, nokan.

yonhon ashi-dai: Also *shihon bashira-dai*. A stand for a nagado-daiko that has four vertical legs. The *yonhon ashi-dai* holds the taiko horizontally at about shoulder height.

yotsutake: Handheld slats of bamboo used as clappers.

Z

za-dai: Also *miyake-dai*. A low stand used to hold a nagado-daiko horizontally at knee height. Often used for the Miyake style of taiko playing.

zelkova: *Zelkovia serrata*. The English name for the *keyaki* tree, which is native to Japan. Traditionally preferred for making *kuri-nuki* taiko, it is increasingly hard to obtain and expensive.

zori: Traditional Japanese thonged sandals similar to the ubiquitous "flip-flops."

References

Davey, H. E. *Living the Japanese Arts and Ways: 45 Paths to Meditation and Beauty*. Berkeley: Stone Bridge Press, 2003.

de Ferranti, Hugh. *Japanese Musical Instruments*. Hong Kong: Oxford University Press, 2000.

Friedman, Robert Lawrence. *The Healing Power of the Drum*. Reno: White Cliffs Media, 2000.

Fromartz, Samuel. "Anything But Quiet." *Natural History*. March 1998.

Hooker, Richard. "The Earliest Japanese Music." http://www.wsu.edu:8080/~dee/ancjapan/music.htm

Lowry, Dave. *Traditions: Essays on the Japanese Martial Arts and Ways*. Boston: Tuttle, 2002.

Maliszewski, Michael, Ph.D. *Spiritual Dimensions of the Martial Arts*. Boston: Tuttle, 2002.

Ochi, Megumi. "What the *Haniwa* Have to Say About Taiko's Roots." Transcript of Plenary Session of First American Taiko Conference. Los Angeles, 1997.

Shikuma, Stan. "Taiko and the Spirit of the Drum." http://www.seattlekokontaiko.org/SKTHistory.html.

Takata, Takeshi. "The Thundering World of Taiko." *Taikology* (Japan). 1997.

Wade, Bonnie. *Music in Japan: Experiencing Music, Expressing Culture*. New York: Oxford University Press, 2005.

TAIKO INFORMATION AND SUPPLIES

Asano Taiko
www.asano.jp

Discover Nikkei Taiko Database
http://www.discovernikkei.org/en/resources/taiko

Kumidaiko.com
www.kumidaiko.com

Miyamoto Unosuke Shoten
http://www.miyamoto-unosuke.co.jp/eng-index.htm

Miyoshi Daiko
http://www.miyoshidaiko.com

Mochizuki Taiko Manufacturing Company
http://www.taikorus.com

Remo, Inc.
http://www.remo.com

Rolling Thunder Taiko Resource
www.taiko.com

San Francisco Taiko Dojo
www.taikodojo.org

© 2005 ROBERT MIZONO

The Spirit of Taiko DVD

Discover the modern taiko movement through the eyes of three generations of artists.

Narrated by Sheila Escovedo.

$24.95. Contact Bridge Media, www.bridgemedia.tv.

STONE
BRIDGE
PRESS

The Way of Taiko by Heidi Varian

An excellent guide for aficionados and performers.

Copies of this book are available to taiko groups for bulk purchase.

For details on pricing, contact Stone Bridge Press.

Stone Bridge Press, P. O. Box 8208, Berkeley, CA 94707 • 1-800-947-7271 • sbp@stonebridge.com